Julia Rocchi's debut *Amen?* is an honest an̲̲̲...
full of deep questions, heartfelt prayers, and sparkling wit for ̲...
Faith is an intensely personal journey, and in *Amen?*, Julia reminds us that no ̲...
our own paths take us, we will never walk alone.

Jennie Adams, author and librarian

Julia Rocchi's *Amen?* is the kind of book that you keep on your nightstand because when you crack it open, you land on the exact prayer, poem, or essay that you need to read in that moment. This gem of a collection both recognizes the harsh realities of our times and inspires hope and action. Brimming with grace, vulnerability, and wonder, Rocchi's offerings are a must-read for people of all faiths who wish to establish or strengthen their spiritual connection.

Michelle Brafman, author of *Washing the Dead*

Julia Rocchi has written a psalter for the post-modern, exhausted age. She reminds us with her essays, poetry, and prayers that humanity has always brought to God our mixed emotions: our joy, our pain, our uncertainty, our anxiety. These prayers name the truth that at times the institutional church has been slow to name: that the truest prayers are those born of the truest emotion, and that certainly the God who loves us holds these in equally loving hands.

The Rev. Megan L. Castellan, Rector, St. John's Episcopal Church, Ithaca, New York

Amen? is an absolute marvel of a book. Julia Rocchi writes with such grace and tenderness, and she is unafraid to ask hard questions, nor to think big. These pages are beating with heart and bursting with imagination.

Audrey Clare Farley, author of *The Unfit Heiress:
The Tragic Life and Scandalous Sterilization of Ann Cooper Hewitt*

Julia Rocchi writes skillfully in two tempos in this delightful volume. In each chapter, she guides fellow seekers through modern questions of faith, using relaxed and often humorous prose. Then she downshifts to a prayerful pace, serving up rich spiritual morsels that are best consumed via slow, mindful attention. The result is Rocchi's great gift to readers: a God who is eminently approachable, yet able and eager to respond to our deepest desires.

Gary Gardner, author of *The Earth Cries Out:
How Faith Communities Meet the Challenges of Sustainability*

To people exhausted by hard lines and polar positions, Julia Rocchi's book is a grace-filled invitation into radical rest. What a relief to meet God and to encounter one another as we are: curious, questioning, fragile, and hopeful.

Karen Wright Marsh, *Vintage Saints and Sinners:
25 Christians Who Transformed My Faith*

Amen? is a poetic, funny, and thought-provoking work for the religious, the spiritual, the non-believers, and everyone in between. Rocchi's beautiful writing and warm humor will make you want to read this book again and again.

Barbara Boehm Miller, author of *When You See Her*

In the meditative, short, personal essays and in the prayer-poems of Julia Rocchi, things unseen and things hoped for cease to be abstract concepts and evolve into what we can grasp through the senses. This book offers a lesson in how to practice our faith and our personal beliefs on a daily basis, through the cycle of the seasons and throughout the inner journey that we all must make as we try to encounter personal happiness and meaning.

Ed Perlman, poet, essayist, reviewer

A thought-provoking, humorful, and human body of work. For the spiritual, the religious, and those among us who aren't really sure, *Amen?* speaks about modern day life—about dating and love, about our culture, environment, and work, about our families—bringing the spiritual back down to earth. Readers will come away feeling connected, inspired, and spiritually awakened.

Jennifer Ryan, bestselling author of *The Chilbury Ladies' Choir*

Amen? is the spiritual journey story I didn't know I needed. With humor, curiosity, and grace, Julia Rocchi reveals the truth about her faith, doubt, and all. This book was a breath of fresh air!

Melissa Scholes Young, author of *The Hive and Flood*

AMEN?

AMEN?

Questions for a God
I Hope Exists

JULIA ROCCHI

To Jamie —
Keep writing — and keep
asking questions!

Julia
Rocchi

LAKE
DRIVE

lakedrivebooks.com

Lake Drive Books
6757 Cascade Road SE, 162
Grand Rapids, MI 49546

info@lakedrivebooks.com
lakedrivebooks.com
@lakedrivebooks

Publishing books that help you heal, grow, and discover.

Paperback ISBN: 978-1957687056
eBook ISBN: 978-1957687087

Printed in the United States of America

Library of Congress Control Number: 2022938610

To my parents, for honoring my questions

Contents

What's It All About?

Way back in 2006, I was an earnest, idealistic twentysomething working my first full-time job and living at home to save money. During the week I pursued a few hobbies and, on weekends, I hung out with my friends. I went on lackluster dates, ate dinner with my parents, and got a head start on experiencing a quarter-life crisis. In short, I was a not-uncommon recent college graduate except, perhaps, for one detail: I regularly attended Catholic mass at my childhood parish.

Now, I do not expect you to gasp at that statement. Being a practicing Catholic is not that unusual. But my religious observance as a young adult *was* somewhat rare among my religion-eschewing peers. "But the abuse scandals," people would say to me. "The misogyny. The hypocrisy of it all." They weren't wrong. I knew I was part of a complicated tradition, one filled with as much sin, pain, and shame as it was with beauty, creativity, and mystery. I stuck with it not only because it was the liturgical language I spoke best but because I stubbornly believed in the idea of small-*c* "church": God embodied as a community of seekers, a group of people who desire to orient their lives around love.

My presence there, however, didn't always mean I was thrilled about religion, especially as a young adult. Even though I ran in slightly more progressive Catholic circles, it was hard to shake the feeling that the church considered my current stage in life unworthy of its time and focus, seeing it instead as a negligible pit stop on the way from teen-focused charismatic worship to middle-aged involvement in family masses and religious education. Out were the overwrought youth conferences and fevered guitar group sessions; in were awkward "young adult socials" that doubled as Catholic singles' meat markets where women outnumbered men four-to-one and those few men were pushing forty.

Eventually I got involved with a local food pantry and soup kitchen where I served meals once a month alongside other "young adult" Catholics who were, on average, fifteen years older than me. And at the invitation of a friend, I joined a vibrant Young Franciscan group (a lay community based on the teachings of St. Francis of Assisi) in downtown Philadelphia, which became the first—and only—young adult activity in that era of my life that focused on contemplation, nurtured participants as individuals, and included only people under thirty.

Getting to this level of participation, though, took a solid year of dogged searching and trial runs. As each fruitless month ticked by, I grew increasingly frustrated that finding connection within the church wasn't simpler. For God's sake (literally), I wanted to be there! I had enthusiasm and willpower and a 1990 Ford Taurus that could take me and at least three other young adults—four if they didn't leave room for the Holy Spirit—anywhere. But I wasn't becoming a nun, nor was I married, nor did I have children. As a result, the church didn't seem terribly interested in me despite my keen interest in it.

I began asking questions. Did my commitment to the church matter? Could my restless energy be addressed or harnessed? Were my inquiries, needs, and desires valid? I felt that no one should ever beg another to stay, to listen, to tend, only to discover that the other cannot—or will not—cross the room to meet the petitioner where they are. Soon I realized I had to channel my frustration somewhere. So I did what any self-respecting millennial did at the time: I went to a blogging platform, selected a template, and began a long run of sincere, navel-gazing entries.

What was my hope with that first desperate stab into the void of the internet? As my earliest posts baldly indicate, I was seeking a community of young adult Catholics who were nurturing an "active and deeply felt" faith beyond the cultural tradition and dogmatic canon. I wanted to meet others who were wondering and wandering. Then, as the years went by and I grew older and—well, not wiser, but wise enough to know I wasn't wiser—I came to understand that I was not alone in my search, both within Catholicism and beyond it.

We receive steady reports about changes in religious affiliation, especially from the Pew Research Center, that as of this writing show almost one-third of U.S. adults now say they have no religious affiliation, a percentage that continues to rise. In Pew's parlance, this group is classified as religious "nones": people who describe themselves as atheists, agnostics, or "nothing in particular." Who's leading this shift? Millennials. My peers. The people I seek out in shabby church halls, the people I write for on the internet, the people I've learned feel increasingly isolated from fellow seekers, doubters, questioners—the body of loving humans that keeps me fumbling for communion even in troubled times.

Back to 2006 for a moment. During that period of frustrated seeking, one night I experienced a dream so visceral that I woke up crying. In the dream I was frantically searching for a beloved youth minister. As I looked for him, I pushed through formless herds of people. Many in the crowd tried to tell me how to feel; I struggled to tune them out. After wandering through several church basement–like rooms, I finally found the minister seated in front of a huge sheet of paper inviting people to write messages and draw pictures. I grabbed a marker and sketched a church with a crooked steeple. I knew what I wanted to add over it: huge, thick, forbidding bars. The thicker, the better. But then I caught my youth minister's eye—his sympathetic gaze, a look that said "I understand"—and I couldn't do it. Instead, I put my head in my hands and sobbed.

All these years later I still feel deep in my chest the frustration, grief, and—unexpectedly—hope contained in that dream. Frustration because I felt no one was listening. Grief because I was leaving the unquestioned church of my childhood and entering a more rigorous and mysterious adult faith. Hope because I couldn't draw the bars. Turns out I hadn't given up on church with a little c, even if it felt like it had given up on me. I didn't want to excise my spirituality, my searching, my own little wick of divine spark flickering inside me. Instead I wanted to participate, ask unanswerable questions, and find others eager to do the same.

In her first book, *Faith Unraveled: How a Girl Who Knew All the Answers Learned to Ask Questions*, the late Rachel Held Evans wrote, "Most of the people I've encountered are looking not for a religion to answer all their questions but for a community of faith in which they can feel safe asking them." This has been my experience as well, and a key reason I've come to believe we are wired for connection with forces greater than ourselves. In my life, that wiring leads to the desire to believe as much as belief itself.

That's what the book you're holding is about: the urge to cultivate a mature and examined relationship with a God we might never fully understand or know. Through essays, reflections, poems, and prayers, I have attempted to transmute my doubt into curiosity and punctuate my faith with question marks. It is the written equivalent of crossing the room to sit beside a fellow seeker, creating a sacred space where a moment ago there was none, and inviting everyone gathered to explore mystery and meaning together. With every question I ask, every prayer I write, every answer I relinquish knowing, I move beyond any one denomination, service, or minister into a liminal space of discovery and transformation. And to every person who raises their hand and says, "That's what I want, too," I say, "Join me. Where we'll end up, I don't know. But let's find out together."

ONE

Do I Gotta Have Faith?

Doubt:

What If I Don't Believe in You?

A Profession of Faltering Faith

My brother told me he was an atheist at the start of a car ride. He opened up the conversation as if he were coming clean. "I want to have faith," he said. "I really do. But I have to be honest and say I don't."

At first I was taken aback. I knew my brother wasn't following any religious doctrine, but I had never stopped to think that might imply his total lack of belief in any deity. I'm a person of faith. A person *with* faith. Imperfect faith, variable faith, doubtful faith—but still faith in a Higher Power.

Then I felt naive, almost narrow-minded. Why had I assumed my brother believed in God? Because he was a good person? Because he expressed morals and values similar to mine? Because believing in God is what our observant Roman Catholic family was supposed to do? Because I believed in God?

Then I wondered: Did his not believing in God make him any less of a kind or worthy person? Did it prevent me from seeing him as a child of God? And if my personal, honest answer to either of these questions was yes, then what did that reveal about me and the quality of my own belief?

I was upset. Really upset. Heart-on-the-floor-mat kind of upset. But I couldn't cry because we were in the car together having this talk and I didn't want to dissuade him from sharing his thoughts. I wanted to hear what he had to say, which turned out to be thoughtful, well-reasoned. My brother had not reached his conclusion quickly or lightly. He had examined all sides and discerned where he stood, a practice to admire in anyone of any tradition.

We went back and forth on various points. To be clear, I wasn't trying to convince him of anything. I believe God works within people individually and each person's spiritual journey is theirs alone. (Plus I'm a terrible debater and fold like a pile of laundry.) Instead, we talked about the constructs of the atheist vs. theist debate. He said he didn't understand why the burden of proof is on the atheists. I said believers and non-believers alike have a faulty premise: that trying to wrap scientific laws around something as intangible, amorphous, and stubbornly unscientific as faith can't help but lead to circular arguments and insufficient evidence.

Then we talked about the meaning of life without ever really using those terms. He said he's in awe of the earth and the wondrous complexity of human existence without needing a Creator behind them. I said that mortality terrifies me and the idea of an afterlife brings a measure of peace.

Then it was my turn to come clean. Really clean.

"Fran," I said, "I have to be honest too. I believe because I want to."

"I appreciate that," he said. "I wish more people would admit it."

Why was I ready to burst into tears then, and for the next 24 hours, and even now as I remember it?

Because questions about suffering, death, and the meaning of life are the waves that rock my little skiff hardest. Because my brother made me realize (admit?) how much I want people I love to share my beliefs. Why, I'm not sure. I think because for all the struggle that believing entails, it ultimately brings me joy, and I want others to experience joy, too.

Because I've never been able to conceive of nothingness without fear creeping in.

Because pondering whether people can end up in a heaven they disavow makes my head and heart hurt.

And because of many other big, daunting, mysterious, sentimental, melancholy, confused reasons I could not articulate right then in the car and still cannot today.

When the waves of questions and doubts threaten to sink me, I recall a memory from my early childhood when my brother and I would play hide-and-seek with our mother. I hadn't yet learned the art of silence, so my mom usually followed my laughter to find me. My brother, three years younger, thought that sitting in a corner, putting his hands over his eyes, and saying "I am nowhere to be found" rendered him invisible. When it was Mom's turn to hide, she played her ace: the ability to remain quiet.

I'd take one floor. My brother would take another. I'd peer in all the spots a big kid could reach. But my brother would play the baby card: a plaintive, repeating refrain of "Mommy, where oo?" that never failed to touch her heart and call her forth from her hiding spot.

Sometimes I think I'm playing the baby card with God. How much easier it feels to wander around in a sad daze, sucking my thumb and tugging at God's heartstrings—"God, where oo?"—until my longed-for subject appears.

But the easiest path is not necessarily the most enriching. Certainly I can ask God where they are, but I too must be out in the open. No covering my eyes. No pretending I'm invisible. If I am going to profess my faith—to declare that I am a person who wants to encounter and experience a force greater than my own self—then I must say it out loud and not in hiding, so that people can hear, disagree, and help me cultivate a mature, examined, freely chosen belief.

My response to the atheist I love may not seem enough to those of you with greater conviction than I. But I could answer only from my heart, and it continues to answer the truest it can.

Suspension of Disbelief

Perhaps there's nothing in the dark to fear.

Perhaps there's nothing in the dark at all.

Still, I prefer a glimmer, at least along the path.

For that, give me a faith that flickers but never quite goes out.

Amen.

Keep on the Wait

How will I know you when I see you?

The darkness shadows your face. The rain obscures your voice. The cold keeps you at arm's length. How will I know if I cannot see? Or hear? Or touch?

People always seem to be asking you this question. From prison cells and upper rooms, along country paths and city sidewalks, in flights of joy and pits of despair—it doesn't matter. We all have to ask. And very few of us seem assured in the answer.

I'll ask again anyway, though. Even if asking appears to waste time, it helps me lead a life that seeks the answer. To me, that's worth the wait.

Amen.

Questions That Come in the Night

Questions that come in the night are drawn in black ink—insistent, bold, stark. Though they may fade from view in broad daylight, their impressions mark my eyelids, faint memories of blank answers.

Trace those imprints on my heart, God, and grant me the dogged faith to follow their loops and squiggles until life's grand design is revealed.

Amen.

Mystery:

What If I Don't Understand You?

"The Universe Wants to Be Noticed"

I believe the universe wants to be noticed. I think the universe is improbably biased toward consciousness, that it rewards intelligence in part because the universe enjoys its elegance being observed. And who am I, living in the middle of history, to tell the universe that it—or my observation of it—is temporary?

. . . I was thinking about the universe wanting to be noticed, and how I had to notice it as best I could. I felt that I owed a debt to the universe that only my attention could repay, and also that I owed a debt to everybody who didn't get to be a person anymore and everyone who hadn't gotten to be a person yet.

—John Green, *The Fault in Our Stars*

Am I living in a way that notices the universe?

Am I living in a way that gazes through both ends of the telescope?

Am I living in a way that pokes around dark corners with bare hands?

Am I living in a way that cannonballs into the pool of human consciousness?

Am I living in a way that admits the possibility of a soul?

Am I living in a way that admits the possibility of oblivion?

Am I living in a way that acknowledges the end of living?

Am I living in a way that digs for the few golden, permanent threads?

Am I living in a way that leaves me choked up, because no matter what I believe, this beauty is undeniable?

On Notice

God, I can't explain
why this world moves me
to tears

maybe because it's so
daring and futile
by turns

but the bare fact remains
it does

so I can only ask
the tears to magnify
my sight

and not obscure it.

Amen.

Warmth in the Stone

Suspend me in that space between "yes" and "fine," between when I choose to choose you and when I consign myself to the glorious calamity of being bound to earth.

I am no blind-faith fool. I see what sits before me; it is a thing and I will name it as such. Yet this thing has a reality beyond its form, and I will name that as well.

Engage me, grubby supplicant that I am with sore knees and wandering attention. Come down from the pedestal, coursing with life, and gather me up.

I began by kneeling to you. I evolved by contemplating you. Let me end by embracing you—flesh around faith.

Amen.

Flaming

The black-clad leaders teach us of an evil
Housed in flame and wrapped in molten ash—
A spirit so engulfed in sin, the light
Around it never penetrates,
Just dies.

Yet black-clad leaders also teach of good
That's carried in swift flight on avian back—
A spirit so essential that its core
Must manifest in purest, whitest flame.

I stretch my palms toward both. I feel the scorch.
A miracle or curse, they burn the same.
Deceptive choice, these tongues. So warm to touch,
Seductive and beguiling . . .

But I pause
And look instead at their reflections.

On one wall, nothingness. Blank.
But on the other, I see my shadow.

Imperfect at first cast, yet tempered as
The light evolves.
In it I see my chances,
I see my possibility,
And with each lick I am more certain
That burns from this absorbing heat
Will heal, not wound—
Will not deny, but give.

I leave my palm outstretched.
I choose.

I live.

Amen.

Free Will:
What If I Don't Follow You?

What Happened When I Stopped Going to Church

One summer I didn't go to church for eight weeks. I had my reasons: travel led to an irregular schedule; I was often visiting people who don't attend church; I didn't want to put on real clothes. Thanks to my Catholic upbringing, I initially felt guilty. I knew I could have made more of an effort—scheduled flights differently, awakened earlier, researched Mass times at local parishes wherever I was. But sometimes I just didn't want to. Turns out it was pleasant not to be on a set schedule, relaxing to spend unbound time with loved ones, comfortable to be pants-less. So I justified my choices, got complacent, forgave myself the absences, and said to God, "I'll be back in the fall." And I was come October. But a funny thing happened on the way back to the chapel: I realized why I was drawn to my traditional spiritual practices in the first place. Here's what I learned.

I appreciate having a regular space for contemplation.
For years I've felt like an anomaly among my broader peer group for attending services at all, much less regularly. When I ask folks about it, they answer with some variation of "Well, church/Mass/services/organized religion doesn't do it for me, so I don't go."

What I learned over my absent summer is that church-going *does* do it for me. The desire doesn't stem from rule-following or a sense of obligation as much as from a need for scheduled contemplative time. I lead a busy and distracted life. My prayer is sporadic. But church—and the routine of attending it—carves out time for me to talk to God.

The Catholic Mass structure in particular speaks to me, and not simply because I was raised on it. At its richest, the Catholic liturgy engages all of a participant's five senses: bold shapes and colors in the sanctuary, the sweet scent of melted wax, well-worn wooden pews, intoned stories and moving music, the bland crunch of communion wafers. The most compelling services I've attended have a subtle theatrical flair. I don't mean that the worship is performative, but rather that the liturgical ministers (clergy, lay readers, musicians, Eucharistic ministers, ushers, and more) have taken great care with every detail, weaving a compelling story the congregant can enter, absorb, and add to.

It also helps that no matter where I go in the world, the format of a Catholic liturgy remains the same, and much like a sonnet, the constraint of a set format allows for internal creativity. The whole experience is designed for contemplation, and while my mouth recites the prayers, my mind feels free to wander among bigger questions and themes, such as "God, where is my place in the world?" and "Where are you guiding me?" There's a tension between familiarity and newness, which leads to discovery.

When I prioritize my desire, the results might surprise me.
I'll be honest: sometimes my lack of attendance that summer was sheer laziness. I was in no mood to make the extra effort. Now I'll be honest-er: sometimes I really did want to go, but I was afraid to offend or inconvenience the people I was traveling with—or worse, I didn't want them to think I was a weird goody-two-shoes.

Here's a case where my fear forestalled potential growth. If I had shared what I wanted at that moment, I would have given my traveling partners an opportunity to respond. Perhaps they would have teased me. Perhaps they would have joined. Or perhaps they would simply have asked why I go, and their question could have prompted a deeper conversation about spirituality in our lives. No matter their response, I would have learned something new about myself and about them. Instead, I let nerves and embarrassment quell the opportunity. Now I know for the future to own what's important to me and see what emerges.

Note to self: beware the easy path.

It's ok not to go occasionally. Clearly, no bolt from the heavens has burnt me to a crisp (yet) for doing that. But not going turned quickly into the easier path, and when I did recommit to attending, I felt weak, flabby, and out of practice, making it harder to get back into the habit. That summer had been the spiritual equivalent of hitting the gym once a week for 30 minutes to sit in the sauna while claiming I'd exercised. The absence of exertion rarely results in meaningful growth. I learned it's worth challenging myself to see what new levels I might attain.

I've been back at church regularly for a while now, and it feels good. I have songs to sing, sermons to contemplate, and a community to befriend. Most importantly, I have at least one hour every week where my mind is focused on something beyond myself. I'm not thinking about emails or writing goals or work projects or dinner. I'm just thinking about God, the state of the world, and my soul: the big questions that even a little time accommodates.

Spiritual Truancy

Free will means I don't have to ask permission. Free will means I don't have to provide reasons. So I won't. I'll come and go as I please. I'm an adult. I dictate my time. My terms.

But of all the terms and time to dictate, why not spend a slice—a sliver, really—on a relationship that is at once the easiest and hardest to maintain? Easy because my partner is already gaga for me; hard because I cannot grasp the enormity of that unseen claim.

No pain, no gain, they say. But the longer it takes to see gains, the more pronounced pain can feel. Still, I will try. Still, I will reach.

Amen.

Bright Spot

Dear God,

I had one moment today where I could have chosen the wrong response. But I didn't. I rose above it. For that brief and brilliant instant, I embodied what you've always asked me to be. Thank you for that grace.

Of course, in the next moment, I plummeted back to earth in spectacular fashion. And I anticipate I will remain flat on the ground for the vast majority of moments going forward as I'm unlikely to achieve a higher plane of being any time soon.

But I saw, however briefly, what I can be, and the lesson leaves the kind of light that lingers for a long time—long enough for me to follow it back to you.

Amen.

Sacreligifice

May the letter of the law not write bonds so tight I can't inhale its spirit.

May the spirit of the law not leave me so light I can't attach to the letter.

Strike this balance in my will, so that I sacrifice weakness but not meaning.

Amen.

Therefore I tell you, do not worry about your life, what you will eat [or drink], or about your body, what you will wear. Is not life more than food and the body more than clothing?

Look at the birds in the sky; they do not sow or reap, they gather nothing into barns, yet your heavenly Father feeds them. Are not you more important than they?

Can any of you by worrying add a single moment to your life-span?

—Matthew 6:25-27

Eyes Up Here

Worriers, I've noticed—mainly because I am one—spend a great deal of time watching their feet. The better to stay on a straight line. The better to avoid a fall. The better to figure out where they are heading.

But worriers, I've also noticed, waste a great deal of time watching only their feet.

God, lift my chin. When the anxiety of who and where and why and what's-it-all-about cloaks my vision, help me blink to clear the fog.

Amen.

Virtual Theology

Game on, God.

You want me. I'm right here. But first you have to track me through multiple levels of increasing difficulty, each with new villains and daunting obstacles and floating manna that racks up points when I jump to grab it.

You want me. I'm on the move. You call me to come back, to rest, to wait for you. But oh no, I'm too clever for that, Player One. Think I'm going to sit here and let you get me? Wrong! Poof! Gone.

You want me. I'm hidden. Keep hacking the vines. Ford the moat. Scale the gate. Leap the chasm. Where will all your daring get you? I'm tucked away in no-man's-land, comfortable, wondering if you can catch up.

Game on, God. It's solely in my power to hit pause and give you a breather. But I don't know if I'm ready to risk that. Because when you catch up to me, will it be game over?

Amen.

Trust:
What If I Don't Trust You?

"The Consequences of My Faith"

From 2016 to 2018 I participated in a program through my parish that radically reoriented my adult faith life. Called Just-Faith, this intensive small-group experience dove into Christian social justice teaching with prayer, study, dialogue, and community immersion to connect participants spiritually, intellectually, and physically with the poorest among us. Or, as I liked to call it, my weekly "rip out your heart and leave it bleeding on the table" class.

Racism, poverty, hunger, climate change, war—the bigger the issues we tackled, the more complex the systems we dissected, the more I awoke to not only the world's injustices but also our global interconnectedness. Placing myself within an intricate web of relationships rather than at the center of an individual island helped me understand my privileges and compelled me to consider how I might manifest God's kingdom on earth, here and now.

Only problem was, I didn't want to heed the call.

One of the program's required texts, *Cloud of Witnesses* edited by Jim Wallis and Joyce Hollyday, included a profile of Martin Niemöller, the German theologian and pastor whose anti-Nazi resistance during World War II and pacifism in the following decades prioritized the teachings of Jesus Christ over the demands of the state. In the interview, Niemöller offered, "I have always said that a pious Christian can be essentially atheist in ultimate commitment. The decisive factor is whether I live the consequences of my faith. Is God my authority? Which God?"

Niemöller's point challenged me. In light of all I was learning through the class, I came to recognize that *declaring* my faith and actually *embodying* my faith were leagues apart. I did not want to be "essentially atheist in my ultimate commitment." But how would heeding the call change me, my actions, my choices, my life? Could I follow this call, the same one that put Niemöller in a concentration camp for seven years, wherever it led?

My issue, I realized, was trust. Trust that God wanted me. Trust that God was with me. Trust that God even existed, because turning my life over to an Incomprehensible Mystery in such a spectacular way seemed silly at best and deadly at worst. And on the smallest and most selfish of levels, I struggled with trust in myself. Could I admit I was powerless alone but powerful with love?

Once I heard the call, I could not unhear it despite my liberal use of cotton balls, pillows, and earmuffs. I confess my steps toward heeding it continue to be halting and timid. But I am learning to trust, every day, at every moment, that the only step I ever need to take is the next one.

At the Forest's Edge

God of the unblazed trail, take me where I need to go. Your signals are clear: walk, pause, listen. Repeat as necessary. I am giving in to giving in, acknowledging your unending wish for us to heed your friendly shoulder tap and follow your confident wave.

As we go, please surround me with new faces and different stories. Introduce me to fellow hikers on the path to conversion. Balance the night sky of my faith with the morning dew of works.

The world has unsettled me with its suffering, but I have not run to the edge of the woods to escape. Rather, I come to be unsettled even more, to face the as-yet-invisible trail, to rejoice at finding your hand in the dark.

Amen.

What's Old Is New

I pretend I am the first
to see the visions
hear the voices
ask the questions

But I know I'm far
from the last
and I know I'm far
from the answers.

I think, though, I've arrived
at a rest stop where others
have paused
because I see their scrawls
on the bathroom walls
and they all say
"keep going"
"you'll learn"
"we promise"

so I will.

Amen.

Overheard: "Stealing Christian music isn't stealing. It's borrowing a prayer. I mean, because if you think about it, God inspired it and basically wrote it."

Moral Relativism

God, are you black and white? Do you exist at the poles? Are you as dogmatic as we have made you?

Maybe it's my imperfect self talking (hoping?), but I believe you are pragmatic and flexible. You can see the forest for the trees—or, in the case of divine indwelling, our souls beyond the sins.

This doesn't excuse bad choices, especially when made knowingly. You're not offering a "Get Out of Jail Free" card. But surely you accept sincere penance and take our intentions into account. You must thrive on our desire to be and do good, God. It must give you hope that one day we goofy mortals will master your master plan of love and forgiveness.

Until that happens, though, thank you for helping us live in shades of gray. From the grayest of them all—

Amen.

Get a Grip

Life is a Slip 'N Slide, and I can't get a grip.

You who can help apply the brakes, help me walk the fine line between acting out of presumption and acting out of trust, so that my every choice aligns with your love.

Amen.

There are already three persons in the Holy Trinity. Don't try to be a fourth.

—Fr. Jim Greenfield

Hand It Over

I could slip it under the door.

I could drop it in the mailbox.

I could fax it from the office.

I could gift-wrap it under the Christmas tree.

I could strap it to a carrier pigeon.

I could seal it in a time capsule.

I could stuff it as a message in a bottle.

I could stow it in an undisclosed location.

Or, I could simply hand it to you.

No matter my delivery method, God, my desire to be in full control must reach your hands eventually if I'm ever to have peace. Just be prepared for it to arrive in separate shipments and over great lengths of time. Thanks in advance for accepting my packages.

Amen.

TWO

So . . . What Is Prayer Exactly?

Relationship:
Are You There, God?

A Conversation We Carry On in Questions

Is prayer as simple as a sentence, as complicated as a curse? Pleas and genuflections, yes, but what about hugs and screams?

What of its tone? Is prayer by nature positive, signaling a flicker of faith where perhaps none is thought to be? Then what about those times when prayer is a wail, a keening moan flecked with spit and blood that twists its way through an unresponsive cosmos toward an unresponsive God?

What of God's response? If my unpracticed antennae cannot detect a reply, how do I build hope? How do I put an ear horn to the most remote canal of my psyche and listen for a greeting in a language I don't speak? How in these silent, ticking moments can I feel heeded, wanted, loved?

What of love? Contemplating it, experiencing it, demonstrating it? When I consider love, do I step toward it tenderly, in awe of its wild nature? When I experience love, do I revel in the sensation? When I show love, do I allow my actions to speak what I cannot articulate and reveal what I cannot describe?

What then is prayer?

It is a conversation we carry on in questions.

Short, Sweet

God, your attributes are expansive, encompassing, and infinite.

Mine are definitely not.

Please help me achieve even one iota of your patience for the next 24 hours. Actually, I'll need your help in this matter for the rest of my earthly life, but I think we should start small, as it's going to be an uphill battle.

Sorry in advance. And thank you. In advance.

Amen.

Baby Steps

Whatever you want me to know, I will learn it.

Whatever you want me to endure, I will sustain it.

Whatever you want me to recognize, I will see it.

Whatever you want me to experience, I will live it.

But promise me, God, that you'll give me the grace to take it one small piece at a time so that the darkness of the universe does not swallow me and the brilliance of your love does not blind me, and I promise you that in the fullness of time we will meet.

Amen.

At Wit's End

A boat was on the shore today;
I thought I would set sail.
No sooner did I hit the waves,
I bore down on a gale.

No sooner than the wind died down,
I chanced upon some rain.
No sooner did the rain dry up,
A sunburn gave me pain.

Aloe helped the burn subside,
Yet still more was in store:
I felt my feet grow wet and saw
A hole in my boat's floor.

No bucket, cup, or extra hat
Could help my filling vessel.
No sooner did the waters breach,
I faced the sea to wrestle.

I put my backstroke to the test
(Though sharks like kicking limbs).
Imagine, then, my pure relief
To end on land post-swim.

So now I'm wet, confused, alone.
My kingdom for a friend!
That's when I realize you're here, too—
Together at Wit's End.

Amen.

God Dropped By

God dropped by today. Sat a spell with me. Said "call your mother." And "don't hate on the neighbors." And "curb the cussing." And "thou shalt have no other gods beside me." And some other stuff.

I forget a lot of it. It's late. I'm tired.

The important thing is, God dropped by. And even though I didn't have a lunch meat tray or coffee cake ready, God stuck around to chat. I appreciate that. Shows a lot of class.

Drop by anytime, God. You're always welcome.

Amen.

Text Me

When my data plan runs over
And my texting wears me out,

When the hotspot starts to cool off
And my thumbs protest and shout,

In those moments when I'm silent
(which means I'm ignoring you),

Send a text of love and healing;
I promise, it gets through.

Amen.

Hosanna

I always thought "hosanna" was a fancy way of saying "Yay! Yippee! You go, God!" But hosanna also translates as "save us," which makes it a cry for help, a call to revolution, and a prayer for power all at once.

For me this puts a different spin on the Christian tradition of Palm Sunday, the biblical and liturgical event that kicks off Easter Holy Week. What I previously viewed as the palm before the storm (I'll let myself out) is actually a boiling point. People are shouting "hosanna!" to Jesus, a radical man the Pharisees despise, in broad daylight at the top of their lungs—praising him, yes, but also appealing to him for healing, strength, and deliverance from oppression. So great is their faith in this man and his message, they allow their hope to overtake their fear, at least for the time it takes for his procession to wind through the city. It's a feeling we know all too well in our times: the desire to celebrate despite uncertainty, the constant struggle against despair.

As I heard parish priest Fr. Jim Greenfield once put it in a homily, "We live life between hosanna and *Eloi, Eloi, lama sabachthani*." The latter were Jesus' last words on the cross, meaning "my God, my God, why have you forsaken me?" So yes, adrenaline will course. Tension will pulse. Our decisions, our dreams, our devotions—all exist between the palms and the passion. Between trust and trepidation. Between revolution and revelation.

No wonder the people shouted. No wonder we still shout.

Palms Up

My God, my God, do not forsake me. Mystify me, challenge me, test me, but don't avoid me entirely.

Yes, I'm begging-bordering-on-beseeching. How can I not? I've been told you're the key to all that's worth having, but I'm not sure what I should do with that knowledge or how I should do it or even if I can do it.

This is my hosanna, God. I'm sitting on the curb, waiting for you to pass me. My palms are facing up. Empty. They're ready for you to fill them. I think. I hope.

Amen.

Goodnight Grace

For the food piping hot, I give thanks to You.
For the folks who have not, I ask of You.
For the day that has passed, I cede to You.
For the dreams coming fast, I rest in You.
For grace upon grace, I trace to You.

Amen.

Presence:
I'm Here. Where Are You?

In Which I Reveal How Bad I Am at Prayer

You, dear reader, might assume that because I have written a book of prayers that I like to pray, or that I'm good at praying, or that prayer comes easily to me.

Alas, none of this is true.

I don't enjoy praying. The chatty voices in my head tend to have one-sided conversations with a Renaissance-era mental picture of a gray-bearded man resting on a cloud, surrounded by fat winged babies and laser-like sunbeams. I check off intentions like grocery list items. I ask for the general concepts I think I should request (strength, patience, world peace) rather than the specific outcomes I want to demand (health cures, jobs, lottery winnings). This is because somewhere along the way I got the notion that (a) you could express only lofty ideas in prayer and (b) others would judge me for attempting otherwise. As a result my brain declares one thing, my heart mutters another, and this creates a din not even a saint could shout over.

But does not enjoying prayer mean I am bad at it? I think the truth is more that I lack a regular, concentrated presence. I am too goal-oriented, too driven by human words in a space and practice that exists beyond benchmarks, beyond language. To relinquish these parameters is to release my puny mind and forgive my even punier capabilities. As Fr. Richard Rohr, teacher and founder of the Center for Action and Contemplation, put it, "Our focus eventually moves from preoccupation with perfect actions of any type, to naked presence itself. The historical word for presence is simply 'prayer.' Jesus often called it 'vigilance,' 'seeing,' or 'being awake.' When you are fully present, you will know what you need to know in that moment."

Presence is prayer. Simple concept, but not an easy act, because God is not easy. As with any relationship, prayer requires commitment, attentiveness, and practice to exist from our steady hearts instead of our racing brains. But instead of wasting energy beating ourselves up over our all-too-human struggles, let's start small. Inhale. Exhale. Recall what good times feel like. Brew a cup of tea. Ask God to sit down. See what happens.

A Sufficient Start

Shhh.

Hello.

I am here.

I am enough.

Amen.

Come Sit With Me

Is it the doorbell ringing? Quick, open the door! It's God coming to love us. Is someone asking us to do something? Here you are! . . . It's God coming to love us. Is it time to sit down for lunch? Let's go—it's God coming to love us.

Let's let him.

—Madeleine Delbrêl, *We, the Ordinary People of the Streets*

Perhaps all God is saying to me is, "Come sit with me. Sit down. Just sit." God pats the picnic blanket, lays out a snack, picks off the stray piece of grass, readies the spot intended for me on the brightly checked cloth. Sun-warmed and soft, the scene beckons me. But I am not ready to sit. Or rather, I am not willing.

God's sincere request—"Come sit with me!"—is not hard to understand, but sometimes it feels impossible to fulfill. How can I sit when I have goals to pursue and tasks to complete, when I have human relationships that require attention and care? Why should I sit on a blanket with a God who is everywhere, around me and within me, just to eat a snack when I could instead be acting on God's word? Surely I know what God wants of me. Surely God wants me just to "do it," whatever I perceive "it" to be.

In my mind, to sit is to surrender, and not in the meaningful spiritual way. It signals rest where I see no room for rest and quiet where I do not wish to listen. If I sit with God, I must *be* with God. Not that being with God requires small talk or logistics. We're not at a cocktail party. It merely requires I show up. But showing up does mean relinquishing something else. Like fun. Ego. Control.

No wonder I continue to decline the invitation.

Yet God keeps asking and patting and putting out snacks anyway. How miraculous that the blanket never fades and the food never stales. How wondrous that the request never changes: "Come sit with me. Sit down. Just sit."

Picnic Prayer

One day, God, I'm certain you'll tire of following me around with your re-folded blanket and your picked-up shoes and the basket full of goodies I never help you lighten. One day you will notice that the sun has set, or the food has molded, or the park where you've been pursuing me has been bulldozed to make way for a housing development, and you'll shrug your divine shoulders and think, "Better luck with the next one" before you head home to put up your feet.

No one can keep up a pursuit this long, especially when there's no reciprocation.

This is how I escape you, right God? I'll pretend I don't see or hear you. I'll pretend you're incapable of loving me. I'll pretend you're pretending, too, but I suspect only I will be none the wiser.

Amen.

To-Don't

Clean bedroom
Clean kitchen
Clean mind
Organize desk
Organize email
Organize thoughts
Figure out rent
Figure out food
Figure out purpose
Hit the gym
Hit the listings
Hit my forehead
Call parent
Call friend
Call for help
Buy milk
Buy tickets
Buy time
Plan party
Plan trip
Plan life
~~Pray~~

Amen.

Frame the Focus

God, help me focus on focusing. May I read the library book I keep renewing. May I write a letter before I check email. May I finish my lunch before I make dinner plans.

Help me remember that it's impossible, physically and temporally, to always be planning for the future, because then I'll never experience the present I so carefully managed into existence.

Keep me in this moment with you—a moment of known past and undetermined future, where calendars dissolve into planetary motion and time is but a machination.

Amen.

In the war of magic and religion, is magic ultimately the victor? Perhaps priest and magician were once one, but the priest, learning humility in the face of God, discarded the spell for prayer.

—Patti Smith, *Just Kids*

This Magic Moment

Magic never begs. The magician, in her hubris, leans on hidden compartments and secret-keeping. Power rests with the hand that wields the wand and the eye that accepts the trick. Belief is complicit.

Not so with prayer. The supplicant, in her humility, senses the audience in the dark and wonders aloud if they are paying attention. Power rests with the palms that face up and the mind that stops minding. Belief is inadvertent.

Face me, God, nothing that I am. Magic's greatest illusion is that of control, but I'll never transform anything the way you can transform me.

Amen.

One Day Your Life Won't Be Like This

One night—somewhere in between working late to prep for a day off, squeezing in reading on the treadmill, planning meals too elaborate for one person, scurrying around giving small tasks great import and important tasks undue smallness—a thought came to me:

One day my life won't be like this.

I thought about my possible children. How many? What color hair? How often will they get stomach viruses? I thought about my possible spouse. How tall? What color hair? How often will we fold fitted sheets together?

I thought about writing, about finally being published, and how I'd drop that juicy tidbit into cocktail hour conversations.

I thought about where I might be living, and what my routine might look like, and what might madden me and what might astound me and what might have fizzled away, and I wondered:

How will I pack lunches and be a listening ear and get my work into the *Paris Review* and help with carpool and retire by 65 and travel the world and call my friends and keep the house clean enough to avoid vermin if my daily existence *now* already overwhelms me?

Then came another thought.

Why not try living this night first, in all its guts and glory?

Then tomorrow night.

Then every night thereafter, until the nights are gone.

Going, Going, Here

God of a million tasks and must-dos and nice-to-haves,

Remind me that stopping—really stopping, as in putting down objects, turning off devices, looking up and around me—anchors me to my present. Ground me in my current dreams and frustrations, as well as in the wisdom that every personal epoch has benefits and drawbacks. Slap me silly until I remember that now is already a good ol' day, simply because the sun rose.

More than anything, grant me the grace of perspective—that for all my annoyances and tired moments, for all my panics and tirades, I am free, the driver of my own destiny, accountable only to myself and to you for what I make of this life.

Amen.

Have a Seat

Sit with me, God, and listen to the quiet unspool across the dusk. Watch the final swoon of day drape around the windows. Feel the solid weight of me beside you, you beside me. Let's be together and nothing less.

Amen.

Stillness:

Is This Thing On?

The Orangutan's Gaze: A Call to Solitude

We saw the crowd before we saw the orangutan. My friends and I had just stepped into the malodorous Great Ape House at the National Zoo, trying to warm up before continuing our wintry Zoolights walk. The gorillas were asleep, draped over hammocks, entangled in limbs, with one stately silverback sleeping upright. But in the far right corner where the orangutans live, a sizable throng was forming.

We saw his jutting jaw before we saw his body. The dusky orange male, looking like a retro shag carpet draped over a coat rack, stood on the ledge against the glass. His fists were raised and pressed at his eye level, and he kept turning his formidable underbite back and forth, back and forth, to survey the buzzing onlookers.

One friend and I horned our way through the crowd and put our foreheads close to the glass. His jaw snapped in our direction; we were in his line of sight. He two-stepped along the ledge to where we stood and solemnly regarded us, his chin down and eyes focused.

I couldn't read his expression. Was he suspicious? Playful? Mocking? Was he wondering why so many bundled humans were pressed against his wall this night? Was he derisive because we couldn't tell time, didn't dress properly for his stinky home, weren't free to play like he was?

Two young boys darted around us and broke the ape's gaze. His jaw turned elsewhere. We walked away. But I found myself thinking about him for a long time afterward. Had he wanted to stay up late? Were we visitors intriguing, annoying, or both? Would he remember tomorrow how today was different? Or had he not noticed any difference in the first place?

At the turn of every calendar year when resolutions promulgate change, clog social feeds, and pit us all against each other in public self-improvement plans, I find myself wanting to be more like the orangutan at the National Zoo. I want to put a wall of glass between my soul and the world's increasing noise. A wall because I need space, silence, structure, solitude. Glass because I also need community, communication, connection, and clarity.

Good thinking, I've come to learn, takes time. Consider the root of ruminate: to chew the cud. True contemplation requires me to return to a thought, look at it from different angles, and let it stew in a dusty corner of my mind where it meets other seemingly unrelated thoughts and then produces wisdom beyond my initial burst of inspiration. That's the point when we do the most honor to our thoughts: when we give them room, when we trust them to live and walk on their own. In doing so we're saying we trust ourselves as well, that we believe ourselves capable of arriving at greater, richer truths.

Here's one such truth I arrived at: solitude scares me. I know I benefit from space and silence. But asking for these things—and making room in my life for them—requires loss. I sacrifice time and much-loved activities. I need willpower and discipline to restructure my days and hold myself to stronger standards. I must say no to myself and others so I can say yes to . . . what, exactly? The unknown quotient intimidates me. I have few expectations around what will emerge. I just know I need to let it emerge, the better to see it, the better to contemplate it.

Here is where my orangutan/glass wall/wisdom of the great apes analogy breaks down, because the orangutan sees many things every day but will never tell us what he's learned. He'll spend the rest of his days in his enclosure, wholly unto himself, and we'll never know what, if anything, made life meaningful for him. This is where I, the human, have the advantage. After standing on the opposite ledge with my fists against the glass, trying to make sense of the colorful babble happening on the other side of the pane, I will get to leave the zoo, share what I saw in captivity, and be freer for it.

Monkey Business

Give me the courage to press against the glass containing me. Squint my eyes to see. Strain my ears to hear. Shape my lips to speak. Curl my hands in tight fists around the truth when it scurries past, and with it firmly in my grasp, help me beat it on the pane so hard I break through into the shocked crowd, now stunned to see in their midst a beast taken aback by its own strength, surrounded by shards of what once was a barrier, ready to lay bare what it heard howling in the night.

Amen.

Flat Tire, Pumped Spirit

God, thank you for flat tires. I drive my life so quickly that a flat tire grounds me; it forces me to sit, think, weigh my options, wait.

Waiting becomes uncomfortable, though. My mind is already on to the next task, the next set of logistics. The disruption of my carefully planned day makes me fret. But while I'm patient with the tow truck, I'm barely patient with you—you who promise always to come, you who don't need to rely on dispatch to find me.

The truth is, I fear the stop. I don't want to sit on the side of the road, alone with my thoughts. Sitting here is vulnerable, watching other cars whizz by, wishing I was out there with them, blaring my radio over the rush of wind.

Because if I don't keep it loud, if I don't keep it busy, if I don't keep it rushed, hurried, and dazed, then I might have to listen to you. I'll have to pay attention when you pull up next to me and offer a spare to get me home. Worse, I'll accept it, and then I'll feel I owe you a favor.

But that's the beauty of your selfless service, God. You give me exactly what I need when I need it most, and then you let me get on with my life, no payment required.

Amen.

All By Myself

God who streams through consciousness—

I pray for the discipline to shush my brain. I pray for the skill to claim the present. I pray for the kind of solitude that doesn't bring loneliness because it brings you instead.

Thank you for the walking hermitage that is a quiet moment. May I visit it often.

Amen.

"Good God in heaven, why don't they have drive-thru Communion?"

—my friend Emily

In the No

Always rushing, always moving. Overscheduled and under-resourced. One activity on the heels of another, each requiring precision in duration and intensity, so that the next event does not hiccup, stumble, or—heaven forbid—fail to occur.

This is my life, God. It has been my life for many years and is entirely of my own creation. Once the approaching brink forced me to scale back, but my commitments have since crept back to previous flood marks.

How am I supposed to fit you in? Where's the time for prayer? Do I have to schedule that, too, amid the commotion?

Am I running away from the silence? ("Yes," says a little voice.)

Am I afraid of what I might hear? ("Definite yes," the voice chirps.)

What could be so bad about a conversation with God? ("Oh, plenty!" the voice volunteers. "You could connect with a greater purpose, uproot your life, respond to a—*aaacccckkkk*.")

That is where I choke my conscience, throw it aside, and make more plans. It's easier that way.

But you know I know it isn't better.

May I practice saying "no" in pursuit of the ultimate "yes."

Amen.

A Hurried Reflection on Patience

Good things come to those who wait. But good long waits come to those who can't wait. Such is cosmic irony. So hilarious. So frustrating.

You know you should wait. Take a deep breath. Live in the moment. Let things unfold.

Screw that. It takes too long.

Instead you drum your fingers on the table and over your keyboards. You stare at your screen(s). You put friends on speed dial to talk you off your manufactured ledge whenever emotions threaten to nudge you onto the hectic street below. You journal your excitement and cloak your anxiety and stock up on ice cream even though it's not on sale. You go to bed late without doing anything of note, and you get up early only to arrive 20 minutes behind anyway. You're afraid to daydream because daydreams aren't guaranteed to come true. You can't help but daydream because it's the only time you feel productive. Are you sleepy or distracted? Confused or illuminated? Dare you trust instinct over intellect in this compromised state? Neither, you decide. So you let all your feelings collide in agonizing slow motion while you watch the clock, waiting for the planned-for, waiting for the wished-for, waiting for the unknown.

Then.

After all this cantwaitcantwaitcantwait . . .

It's over. Done. Whatever it turned out to be. The flush of discovery fades. The zing of newness subsides. Reality re-forms around what used to make you toss and turn. You're left wondering why you rushed it in the first place. You wonder why it took so long yet went so fast. And instead you ask—

Was it worth the frenzy?

Was it worth missing the meantime?

A Good Wait

God, see me through this, or I will explode all over this room in tiny messy bits that are likely to stain the carpet. I don't want that. You don't want that. Let's work together, shall we?

Amen.

Rest/Stop

Hit the brakes. Take that exit. I need a vending machine stocked with chocolate and popcorn and a restroom filled with new mattresses and down pillows.

I've decided, God—as much as it's in my power to decide such things—that I am done. No more. Time for balance. Time for equilibrium. Time for a routine, for mealtime, for all-around stay-puttedness.

Sit with me on the bench near the curb. We'll leave the car parked, locked. Let's watch the other travelers pull in, pull out, pull over. Show me what contentment looks like in the afternoon sun.

Amen.

Silence Speaks Loudest

Amid cackles and crackles and reverbs and pings,
Cloaked in echoes and static and racket and rings,
Next to babble and bellows and ruckus and dings,

I sit still to listen . . . and learn my soul sings.

For I could not hear it above all the noise—
Could not heed the sorrows, could not share the joys.

But now I'm aware (since having begun)
That souls tend to whisper at the tops of their lungs.

So beyond all the clatter and clamor and fuss,
Over the fanfare and shouting and muss,
My soul quiets all with a "shhh" and a sigh—
God's voice not on mute, but instead amplified.

Amen.

To Lie Fallow

Around the end of every year, when daylight drips away and cold creeps in, when the heft of previous months have worn my shoulders sore, I find I want to lie fallow. Plowed but unsown. Arable but uncultivated. Remembered but ignored.

By that time every year, I have scheduled a thousand appointments, completed a million tasks, and dashed about in a billion circles, but I have scarcely moved an inch on whatever I said I would prioritize at year's start. So I vow to begin again. To strip away non-essential distractions. To allow my brain, body, and soul the rest of a tired, overworked field that has no nutrients left to give.

Yet shortly after this time every year, I have an aggravating habit of fencing off a plot of land, then buying the neighboring farm. "SPACE!" my doer side shouts, and before my better judgment catches up, my mind has started twirling in *Sound of Music*-esque circles around the fresh new territory, convinced that this time, this year, the results will be different.

Every year, I am wrong.

I am tired of doing. I am tired of giving. Unfortunate, really, given the state of our world and all that requires doing and giving. But if the nutrients aren't there, how can I hope to share them? How can I keep sticking seeds in spent soil and watering weak sprouts, begging them to grow into something bigger than what I've put into them?

In *Writing Down the Bones*, author Natalie Goldberg says, "Our senses by themselves are dumb. They take in experience, but they need the richness of sifting for a while through our consciousness and through our whole bodies." Am I willing to trust the future potential yield of a rejuvenated mind and heart, or will I instead let fear—fear of failure, fear of inadequacy, fear of not growing anything at all—drive my output? True, I'm not guaranteed results from a fallow period. But I will almost certainly fail if I don't rest the ground where I plant.

Leave Me Alone

Leave me alone, God. Let me be. I am dormant, I am dead, I am no longer home and awaiting your call. I'd say I moved on to greener pastures, but let's be honest— right now green is the last thing I have the energy to be.

I want to be uncropped. Unplucked, unpicked, unharvested. Left beyond the borders of your consciousness so that my own consciousness can let earthworms glide through it, uninhibited and uninterrupted.

Un. I want to be un. Just un.

Sow later, God. I promise you bounty if you leave me unbound.

Amen.

A body at rest will remain at rest unless an outside force acts on it. And a body in motion at a constant velocity will remain in motion in a straight line unless acted upon by an outside force.

—Newton's First Law of Motion

In other words, run run run run run run runrunrunrun THUNK.

A Body at Rest

I ask for answers. You give me better questions.

I ask for affirmation. You give me confidence.

I ask for reassurance. You give me courage.

I ask for progress. You give me patience.

I ask for change. You give me evolution.

I ask for success. You give me rest.

I ask for the strength to be at peace with and in this gift-filled moment, suspended between the asking and the granting. Perhaps you'll give me contentment?

Amen.

Exhaustion Pipe

God, can you hold off on being the rock of salvation for a moment and be a pillow instead?

A firm pillow, so that my integrity is sound and my moral backbone intact. Yet also soft, so that my tossing and turning, my questioning and wandering, is invited and accepted.

From the setting sun to the rising dawn, I look to you for peace and comfort. Ease my body and my mind. As my wildest dreams and darkest nightmares play out with you against my cheek, may I rest assured you are leading me toward a waking state.

Amen.

Sunday Kind of Love

I want a Sunday morning with jazz on the radio and bagel crumbs in the bed, an open window and no reason to get up, the paper finished, but not my dreams.

Keep the Sabbath holy, you ask of us. Mark this day as different. Sacred. A cycle bound for peace and reflection.

Help us put tumult to bed this day. As we fall into your comfort, shape our loose limbs into an embrace, no matter how tangled, and let us rest there, quiet, until you call on us to rise again.

Amen.

Discernment:
Now What?

A Parable for Our Times

The woman went to her cubicle to send an email to her loved one.

The first email she sent was rushed and short. It was filled with typos and emojis. The receiver did not know what to make of it, and so did not respond.

Dismayed at not hearing from her loved one, the woman sent a second email. This one was overthought. It was filled with words that did not match her feelings. The receiver misunderstood the email, and sent back a short and unsatisfactory response.

Now the woman decided to send a third email. She sat down, examined her heart, and typed its truth on the screen. She sent it with the knowledge it was honest. And the receiver finally grasped her message and responded in kind.

Why don't we speak in parables anymore? Wine and seeds. Vines and sheep. Coins and sons. All common elements of a past world, all used to illustrate bigger, more mysterious concepts. We don't teach each other in such subtle ways today. Are our cultures too complicated? Is our attention too shallow? Or do we of the modern world perceive ourselves as above these deceptively simple tales—beyond mystery and beyond questions?

I crave a parable for our times. I want a crucial truth about our mysterious God broken down into something that's a little more than metaphor and told to me in a sing-song voice that lulls me into understanding. Because no matter what the truth is, I believe what God wants most is for me to say, "Tell me a story," and then listen, chin in hand.

Parable of the Need

God of yarns, tell me a story.

Give me a hero and a villain. Outline the conflict, lay out the quest. Lead me through three acts. Grant me a happy ending. For the world is an obstinate place that refuses spooling into a single thread, and the enormity and breadth of its subplots can overwhelm even the most dedicated reader.

Show me the page that matters most in this moment. Give me a hint how this chapter could end.

Amen.

Live a life worthy of the calling you have received.

—Ephesians 4:1

But what if I didn't pick up?

Missed Call

Sorry, God, can't hear you.
Too much traffic behind me.
My battery is dying.
I'm caught in a wind tunnel.

(What you hear me say:
Too much choice in front of me.
My faith is flickering.
I'm trapped by indecision.)

God of the universal switchboard, stay on the line until I hear you. Discernment sits at the intersection of wisdom and honesty. Help me find my way there, where we'll talk some more.

Amen.

I know that you believe you understand what you think I said, but I'm not sure you realize that what you heard is not what I meant.

—Robert McCloskey

Answering Machine

We need to have a chat, God.

Nothing is clear right now. No-thing. I tried to figure things out. That didn't work. Then I tried to not figure things out. That didn't work either. Now I'm trying to figure out how not to figure things out so I can stop trying to figure things out. Surprise . . . IT'S NOT WORKING.

How are you calling me to act? How are you calling me to love? How are you calling me to decide? How are you calling me to move? If I can't connect with you on even one of these questions, how do you expect me to address them? Are you calling me at all?

Maybe I haven't handed over the confusion to you as completely as I thought. But maybe I did hand it over and you dropped the ball. Or maybe you handed it back to me and I dropped the ball.

I don't know because I can't seem to tune into your explanation. Mind, heart, body—all are too noisy. Too frustrated. Too worn out with beating ceaselessly against the rocks.

So just answer me this, God—are you listening?

Amen.

In One Ear

In one ear and out the other—
Why can't words just stay there?
How am I supposed to learn
When they become mere air?

I hear the phrases and the voice
But don't absorb intent.
No wonder, then, confusion reigns
When ears are fickle vents.

The trick, I've heard, is not to hear,
And listen hard instead.
A simple concept, to be sure—
Yet harder done than said.

So dear God, I turn to you
To close my mouth, not mind.
Perhaps I'll even heed you more
And then respond in kind.

Until then, may the whistling wind
Between my ears die down.
Silence amplifies the truth;
I want to hear the sound.

Amen.

The Day I Had a Revelation

The revelation occurred as I was chugging through my to-do list. It didn't come via lightning bolt or earthquake. No heavenly chorus or sudden blindness. It was not about my past or future. It did not bring answers or invite questions. It was a fact, simply stated: *Everything is as it should be.*

The revelation stood there with its head cocked to one side, hands in its pockets, rocking slightly on its heels. It didn't want acknowledgment; it just wanted to sit with me as a bruising weight lifted off my heart and a comforting solidity, like being under three wool blankets in winter, settled over me instead.

Secure in that warmth, I understood it signaled rightness. Not right in the sense of *correct*; right in the sense of *good*. Moreover, it did not signal that everything was perfect or happy or easy. But it did show that I was surrounded and buoyed, supported and believed in—in short, loved.

Poet and philosopher Kahlil Gibran, in his poem "On Love" in *The Prophet*, wrote "When you love you should not say, 'God is in my heart,' but rather, 'I am in the heart of God.'" That's where my revelation put me: square in the heart of God, to-do list and all.

Jailbreak

Spirit of subtlety and strength: Dismantle the cell that has welded itself around my faith and left me no room to swell with love for you. Rip off the padlock. Reach in and pull out what's left of my groggy, soggy soul. Resuscitate at will. Remind me what you and I are capable of when we're in cahoots.

Amen.

Worries

How do you know when your logic has come full circle? When you're still at war, not peace? When you missed the exit for arrival at your conclusion?

I for one don't know. If I did, I wouldn't have turned my poor brain into a worry stone.

God of perspective, help my puny mind rest from wrestling with mystery. Direct it instead to solving the solvable. Rub off the soot that clouds the once-clear glass of my lantern and shine it on a path worth following.

Keep me from worrying myself so smooth that I slip away for good.

Amen.

What to Pray When You Don't Know What to Do Next

Suscipe

Take, God, and receive all my liberty,
my memory, my understanding,
and my entire will,
all I have and call my own.

You have given all to me.
To you, God, I return it.

Everything is yours; do with it what you will.
Give me only your love and your grace,
that is enough for me.

—St. Ignatius of Loyola

When I first learned about the Suscipe, a Catholic prayer written by St. Ignatius of Loyola, I read it as a prayer of thanksgiving—a saint-backed example of what you pray for when life is good. But upon more research, I learned it's part of St. Ignatius' Spiritual Exercises, a four-stage process designed to enrich people's experience of God in their daily lives.

In particular, the Suscipe—translated from Latin as "take"—prepares the petitioner for discernment, which is essentially decision-making in the presence of God. As author Amy Welborn writes in *The Words We Pray*, "the word [discernment] implies not coming up with a new idea completely out of our own creativity, but clarifying things so that we can see and understand something that's already in place: what God wants us to do."

When I'm faced with a big choice and stymied about what to do next, I put myself in the mindset of the Suscipe. Reflecting on these words relaxes me about immediately having the answers while it also deepens my responsibility to consider routes I'm ignoring, fearing, or not recognizing—yet. Ultimately, though, the prayer balances free will with divine guidance, offering a powerful reminder that I'm never in this alone, and that in itself is a gift.

Suscipe, Inverted

You took, God, and received all my demands,
my complaints, my discomfort with mystery,
my entire willful spirit,
all I grip and refuse to release.

I forget you've given all to me.
To you, God, I owe credit.

Everything should be yours; I'll do with that what I will.
But give me (please) your love and grace anyway
so I learn it is enough.

Amen.

Dilemmas and Decisions

Chocolate or vanilla. Left or right. To be or not to be. Every day brings new choices, and it's up to us to decide which path follows you.

Ok, "chocolate or vanilla" is flippant. If only all decisions had low stakes. It's just that we confused mortals become so wrapped up in our human dreams—regrets, hurts, woes, moral crises—that our vision clouds, and we end up running around without thinking, bumping into one another and leaving bruises.

I wish every decision I made was the right one. I wish the path were immediately clear. I wish I trusted myself (and you) enough to follow my gut when the answer *is* clear. Because decision-making hurts. It requires sacrifice and vulnerability. It confronts a person with old wounds and new fears. No wonder we shy away from it. Better to stick in ruts we know; they are safer, and more convenient.

God, be with me in the figuring out. Lead my discernment. Compel me in rare quiet moments to heed your guidance. Help me remember your grace is present even in the wrong choices and that peace always follows turmoil. Bless all my outcomes, yes, but more so the decisions that precede them.

Amen.

Two Roads Diverged (Contrary to Robert Frost)

Two roads diverge each day I live,
And all those days, my steps I choose.

I try considering options all—
What's right for me? What's best by you?

But thoughts converge with blinding speed:
Should I have stayed? Should I have veered?

That's when I hear your whispered shout:
I never ask you live in fear.

Doubt, confusion—each will come.
But never fear when you're with me.

God, I wish I could travel both
If just to know what might (or will not) be.

Still, two roads diverge each day I live, and I—
I'll lead the life you freely give.

Amen.

What Comes from Silence

Insight, I am slowly understanding, does not come gilded or
bedecked with bows. It does not spring forth fully formed. It
does not arrive even large enough to see—it's more an
accumulation of specks on the curtain of silence around me. I
sense I must draw the curtain tighter, but not too tight, just
enough to light the dust.

God of the unpretentious revelation, I will gather the
breadcrumbs as you drop them. I will guard them. Arrange
them. And when the time is right, I will serve them as a feast
made holier by its quiet preparation.

Amen.

Why do we love the sea? It is because it has some potent power to make us think things we like to think.

—Robert Henri

On Empty

I praise you, God, for my emptied mind.

The situation was dire before you intervened. Jotted lists bled into an undecipherable puddle of ink. Crumpled sticky notes clogged the pipes. Reminders, suggestions, options, edicts— all jockeyed for position at my top of mind and threw right hooks so sharp that I lost gray matter in the melee.

But thanks to naps, tides, books, and other holy stillnesses, all those nagging, nattering nothings are back on their shelves, where they will pout but not come closer.

Such is your restoration of a beleaguered brain. Quick! Write what you want me to know before my own words break free again.

Amen.

Forward/Inward

We all sit on the spectrum of contemplation and action, in constant tension between moving forward and growing inward.

Make me like the tree I watch from my window. It extends its hidden roots and grips the earth so its rustling branches can come closer to scraping the sky and finding the truest blue.

Without roots I am weak. Without branches I am stagnant. Help me nourish both.

Amen.

THREE

What About Love?

Divine Love:

Is It Possible to Love Love?

God So Loved the World, God Gave Us Love

Not just any love either, but big love. Brimming love. Brazen love. Love that walks upright and speaks without thinking and goes where it pleases.

Love that has its own backbone, sturdy and beautiful, that it happily drapes with our stumbling words and deeds so it can go out in public and be recognized, even in its imperfection.

Love that raises an eyebrow when we throw fits and leans against the door with arms folded, patiently waiting for our tantrums to subside so it can start on the real work of fixing things.

Love that comes inside covered with grass stains and mud splotches, ecstatic at all the adventures to be had and positive there is time enough to have them.

Such is the love God gave us.

Such is the love God asks us to live.

Labor of Love

Half-metered sonnets, un-scored symphonies, paintings still wet, strings of screenplay quotes, a thousand stellar ideas that haven't seen the light of day . . . these expressions of love all clatter in my head, wishing to testify to a greater, more mysterious truth but lacking the courage.

Coax it out, you say. It does the world no good when left unsaid, undone. But what if these visions vanish when the light hits them? What will be left?

Help me trust the integrity of revelation. Help me believe in my own lucidity. Help me see that Love is already a work of art, and all it requires is for me to unveil it.

Amen.

Love Bugs

My love is impatient. My love is frustrated. My love doesn't want to be kind or understanding or polite. My love wants its way. Which probably means I don't have love, I have agita.

If my love isn't formed, then what? Maybe I first have to imagine and envision and act it—even if I don't fully feel it—to summon the gift into a solid state.

Maybe I do already have love and it's young—a sprouting emotion searching for a crack in the sidewalk where it can stretch toward the sun through the pavement's ragged edge.

Or maybe my love is old, well-formed and aged, resting on the sagging couch watching me come and go, knowing that at some point I will wear myself out and collapse beside it so we can finally have a real conversation about necessary truths.

God, help me find peace in my partial knowing. Bear with me in my childlike ways. Teach me that love is patient, love is kind, and love can be—will be—me.

Amen.

The Autograph of God

To a God in need of more publicists,

I have written you fan mail and hate mail alike, but no matter what I write, I receive the same response: a glamour shot (obviously photoshopped) with the standard line, "Thanks for getting in touch! I love you! GOD."

I bet you write this to everyone.

I mean, come on. You can't possibly love every person who tries to contact you, every person who wants your ear, your time, your help. To adore and cherish every single correspondent requires inexhaustible patience and forgiveness. Who has that kind of energy anymore?

I can't help but feel you've written something between the lines. That if I hold the picture opposite a mirror or before a black light, or leave it in the sun for a few days, a message will appear in lemony ink that provides many more details, instructions, and answers. Surely "I love you" is not, on its own, enough.

Right?

Write back soon and let me know.

Amen.

Harden Not My Heart

God of high callings, release my expectations
of myself
of others
of you
but mainly myself.

Being hard on my heart does not make discernment easier.
Deriding my gifts does not permit me to give them more
freely.
Demanding too much of love does not help me feel it
or share it
or build it.

Dismantle these expectations and hurl them into the dark
night. They will clang and clatter as they go, but in the silence
that follows I'll learn the truth
be it sad
be it joyful
be it yours.

Amen.

Love Alone

To be lonely is to be without company. To feel cut off. Apart.

To be alone, however, can mean to be incomparable. Unique. Separated from others, but in a way that distinguishes.

How fitting that you alone ensure I will never be lonely. You alone are love.

Amen.

Owner of a Lonely Heart

Every day you write. Every day you call. And every day I shrug you off, waiting for a better offer.

I suppose then I am lonely by my own design.

God, help me perceive the love before me. Help me receive it. Help me believe it. Help me relieve myself and others of the pressure to be everything always. It's a standard none can achieve except you.

Amen.

Awesomesauce

Awe is wonder. Awe is dread. But awe is also veneration: to honor what sits before you, to admire all its facets, to defer to where it can lead you and what it can teach you.

Why then are we scared to be awed? Why do we shy away from acknowledging awe and inspiring it? Why do we not look at the daily miracles at work in our hearts and minds and say, "this is worth expanding; this is worth revering; this is worth exalting"?

Force of awe beyond our reckoning, bury the nasally voice that says we are not worthy and turn the knobs way up on the symphonic chorus that says we are. For if we listen to beauty, we become it.

Amen.

Love of Other:

How Serious Are You About the Golden Rule?

Love Rays

When I was five years old, I asked my parents where babies come from. After what I'm sure was a panicked beat they answered, "When two people love each other very much, their love comes together and makes a baby." So for the next few years, my conception of conception was that love rays shoot out of a couple's chests, collide in between them, and form an infant floating in space.

Now as an adult I know the biological process of creating human life, but a broader theological question remains: Can I love something, anything, so deeply and so sincerely, that I give it a life beyond its abstraction? For example, can I love a goal into an achievement? Can I love inspiration into art? Can I love an acquaintanceship into friendship or romance? Can I love the act of loving so much that I give love consciousness?

Here is about when my head explodes with this train of thought, so I'm handing it to you. Can focusing on love itself, rather than the objects of it, become a self-fulfilling mission? And does focusing on love protect us from playing God, instead helping us play human in our cracked, reflective, and occasionally brilliant glory?

Cuppa Love

"Love one another as God has loved you." Golden in its simplicity. Direct in its order. Impossible much of the time.

But what if I sit at a diner counter and see love before me as a steaming cup of coffee, waiting for me to wrap my hands around it, cradle it, sip it? What if I pass the cup? Fill another one? Make a fresh pot and invite others to sit with me? We'll line the diner counter together, each with a cup before us, warm and energized—not thinking about the menu, not thinking about the check, just savoring what's before and within us.

Amen.

Be who you are and be that well.

—St. Francis de Sales

Come Out, Come Out, Whoever You Are

We are made in your image and likeness.

Does this mean you have eyelashes and a tendency to bite your nails? Probably not.

Does this mean you are every color and no color, each creed and any creed, both sex and sexuality? Getting warmer.

Does this mean you contain the spectrum of human possibility at its best and finest? Definitely.

And what about us? Are we omnipotent and omniscient, aware of what's churning in our fellow humans' hearts? Eh, not so much.

Does our finite understanding bump up against infinite permutation? Hmm, closer.

Are we 7 billion refractions of you, with more courage, compassion, and capacity to love within us than we will ever grasp or fulfill? Bingo.

God, be with those who are learning about themselves yet afraid to share their self-knowledge with others for fear of rejection, reproach, and recrimination. Also be with those who are angry and confused for reasons they cannot name; help them comprehend and accept your multitudes.

Remind us that you have so much love in your being that you pour it into us to keep from exploding, and help us sharpen the endless facets that complete your prism.

Amen.

New Heights

When my voice is weakest, all the more reason to shout your praises from the rooftops, for you have reversed the curse of Babel.

You have shown us that the human predilection to develop language (nearly 7,000 spoken ones at last count) does not surpass our ability to be understood. You have granted us comprehension beyond words, and through it, solidarity.

Love is not a foreign substance, but the indestructible mortar for a universal church. Help us be the bricks for a new tower—one that reaches you in the heavens—and give us one voice to sing as we build.

Amen.

"I Know What Love Is"

June 19, 1937

Dear Cedric,

A strange thing happened to me today. I saw a big thundercloud move down over Half Dome, and it was so big and clear and brilliant that it made me see many things that were drifting around inside of me; things that related to those who are loved and those who are real friends.

For the first time I know what love is; what friends are; and what art should be.

Love is a seeking for a way of life; the way that cannot be followed alone; the resonance of all spiritual and physical things. Children are not only of flesh and blood—children may be ideas, thoughts, emotions. The person of the one who is loved is a form composed of a myriad of mirrors reflecting and illuminating the powers and thoughts and the emotions that are within you, and flashing another kind of light from within. No words or deeds may encompass it.

Friendship is another form of love—more passive perhaps, but full of the transmitting and acceptance of things like thunderclouds and grass and the clean granite of reality.

Art is both love and friendship, and understanding; the desire to give. It is not charity, which is the giving of Things, it is more than kindness, which is the giving of self. It is both the taking and giving of beauty, the turning out to the light the inner folds of the awareness of the spirit. It is the recreation on another plane of the realities of the world; the tragic and wonderful realities of earth and men, and of all the inter-relations of these.

I wish the thundercloud had moved up over Tahoe and let loose on you; I could wish you nothing finer.

Ansel [Adams]
(From *Letters of a Nation*, edited by Andrew Carroll)

The poet in me loves encountering a surprise image, an unexpected comparison that jolts me to attention and prompts a fresh insight. Photographer Ansel Adams' thundercloud is just such an image, taking a weather event usually painted in dark, menacing terms and transforming it into a light-pierced revelation.

Every time I read his letter, I am standing with him on a peak in Yosemite watching the cloud descend, and contemplating this view of a physical landscape illuminates an interior one for me. How well I think I know the domes and valleys of my heart, the contours of my capacity to love. But then the sunlight shifts, the shadows flip, and a different slant reveals that I always have new angles to explore and new depths to discover.

If love is indeed "the turning out to the light the inner folds of the awareness of the spirit," then Adams has captured a vivid, evocative frame: Love is not about relationships, but is relationship, not simply the connection but the way we are connected, accounted and cumulative.

Wish Me Nothing Finer

If you meant love to be solitary
You would not have bothered creating us.

You would not have given us thoughts.
You would not have given us voices.
You would not have given us a world to wander through,
companions to encounter,
or any knowledge of you.

But you did give us all these things
free of charge
with a simple hope:

That we send our gifts back out in iridescent rays,
filtered through our inevitable imperfection,
and live for the revelatory moments
when the thunderclouds split
and we—quick!—shield our eyes
and remember what it feels like to be warm.

Amen.

Love Is for the Weak

Let us love, since our heart is made for nothing else.
                                    —St. Therese Lisieux

Love is for the weak, who cry from bed for water though the nightstand holds a glass.

Love is for the hunted, who chew their cuds in open glades, forgetting they are prey.

Love is for the brittle, who snap at slightest pressure, crack, and clatter to the floor.

Love is for the wounded, who slump against the barricades and weep to lift the flag.

Love is for the dim, who do their homework every night and always get it wrong.

Love is for the lost, who dropped their map 10 miles back and can't recall the turn.

Love is for the snitch and the stool pigeon, the turncoat and the tattletale, the liar and the loser. It is for the snookered, the cynical, the spooked. The shivering and the shabby, cranky and conceited, bloated and boorish. Love is for the slack-jawed, cross-eyed, weak-kneed, yellow-bellied, chicken-livered folks. For the bland. The forgettable. The forgotten.

Love is for those who say they don't want it, and for those who won't say they need it.

Love is for anyone but the whole.

Let Us Love

I can never love as you love—a saturating, inundating love we call "love" only because we have no other word to capture the deluge. No, I am merely a chipped cup, long emptied of unmemorable contents, now gathering dust in a neglected cabinet, alone except for the cobwebs.

But even from this forgotten corner, pour out of me what I don't think I have. Let me sit filled, because I'm not alone, not really. Millions of hands jostle just outside the cupboard, blindly groping for something, anything, to slake their thirst, and all I need to do is inch closer and nudge open the door.

Amen.

Pre-K teacher: Where do you find love?

Student 1: In your mouth.

Student 2: In your heart. And your heart is in your chest. Kind of by your trachea.

This One Goes Out to the Ones I Love

I pray for babies who grasp at mobiles, blow raspberries, and sing themselves to sleep.

I pray for kids who imagine pirate ships in their backyards and set sail before dinner.

I pray for adults hell-bent on changing the world, because to believe it is to do it.

I pray for friends who, through stellar example, challenge you to become your best.

I pray for couples who grasp what they've signed up for and proceed with enthusiasm.

I pray for parents, pending or practiced, as they pop buttons and aspirin in equal measure.

I pray for elders who graciously impart what they know to make room for new lessons.

I pray for souls who have left our sides but not our memories.

Amen.

For What the Bells Toll

Extra kisses and damp cheeks. Tissues tucked in sleeves.

Fingers locked together. Arms draped across shoulders. Bare feet.

Spontaneous cheers. Too-loud laughter, punctuated with snorts.

Perfume lingering on well-worn clothes. Wafting aromas of hot food and guests.

"I love you" rich and round in our mouths. Easy to let slip.

Celebrations do not have to be orchestrated events or lavish spectacles. Joy and love are often messy—muddy, grass-stained, sticky. And even when they do come prettily packaged, the ageless heart they wrap tugs at the ribbon, eager to be indiscriminate.

Help us be reckless with our love and brazen with our joy. As bells ring riot, not bothering with the hour, not knowing who hears what or when, so too should we fling our arms open to life's greatest mysteries and accept all comers. Now is no time to be stingy.

Amen.

FOUR

How Do I Define
the Relationship?

Friendship:

What Will Make Me the Best of Friends?

42 Thoughts on Friendship

1. I want to know about your day and your dreams, your longings and your lunch.
2. Let's avoid festering. Also wallowing. Certainly no stewing. Tell me when you are mad at me, and I'll do the same in return so we can get on with the most important (and more enjoyable) business of liking each other.
3. Let's be patient with our learning curves.
4. Let's be compassionate toward each other's mistakes and our own.
5. Our love will never be unconditional because we are human. Still, it's good to have goals.
6. I don't wish you happiness. I wish you contentment: a comfortable assurance that your life is your own and that it satisfies you.
7. What do you see as your purpose on this earth? Can you articulate it? How can I help you achieve it?
8. I wish you believed in something bigger than yourself.
9. Wait for me!
10. Please don't ever fall so far behind or go so far ahead that we lose each other.
11. What grounded our friendship when it began? What grounds it now?

12. If we met for the first time today, would we be friends?
13. What if we grow apart? Then what?
14. Can we fix this? Do we want to?
15. Sometimes, you are really selfish.
16. Sometimes, I am really selfish.
17. You take more than you give.
18. Do you need me at all?
19. I miss you.
20. Thanks for letting me be myself.
21. Thanks for bringing out my best self.
22. Thanks for putting up with me.
23. Are you listening?
24. Thanks for listening.
25. Grow up.
26. Branch out.
27. Get over it.
28. Man, friendship sucks sometimes.
29. Cry with me?
30. I don't always like you.
31. I'm here for you in spite of myself.
32. You're here for me, but I'm still lonely.
33. I wish I had what you have.
34. Seriously?
35. Remember that time...?
36. Growing up is hard. So is living. I'm glad you're in the trenches with me.
37. If I could shut out the world for a day and settle into time with you, I would do it in a heartbeat.
38. Come over. Wear sweats. Bring ice cream.
39. Deep breath. Count to ten. You can do it.
40. I'm proud of you.
41. I believe in you.
42. I love you. Always.

Do You Recognize Yourself?

When you look at me, red of cheek and sputtering of speech, do you spot your own frustration? When you listen to me, gushing with glee and bubbly in spirit, do you share my rarefied air? When you drape your arm across my shoulders, tensed and drooped, do you follow me into the pit not to stay, but to understand enough to hold my hand in the dark?

I already know the answer. I ask aloud because I sometimes forget that you have said yes to me, that I have said yes to you, and that together we've said yes to a connection greater than ourselves. By asking if you are indeed my friend, I remember I am called to be one to you.

Amen.

A friend is one who walks in when others walk out.
—Walter Winchell

Friended

You may know me through and through, God, but you're not the one who picks up the phone or mails a card or knocks on the door to remind me of who I am.

That role is reserved for my friends, your terra firma ambassadors, who challenge and reward me—sometimes in the same moment. For them, I ask you, God:

Turn more water into wine so we can linger over it together.

Grant us stamina for long conversations and patience for radio silence.

Keep us secure, but not safe; a little dangerous thinking with partners in crime keeps the world on its toes.

Thank you for putting people in my life whose wrinkles I can imagine but will never notice, because I know we will grow old together.

Amen.

Friendly

God, you loved us so much, you gave us friends to prove it.

Thank you for overflowing my life with bright souls: people who brim with hope and energy, who strive to improve the world, who make time, who make jokes, who make me see you.

May I be that kind of friend for them. May I do so with honesty, responsibility, and affection. May I lavish love in your name.

Amen.

On the Occasion of My 10-Year High School Reunion

I accidentally wore purple to my 10-year high school reunion—an unconscious pull from the closet that reflected four years of purple and gold everything at my all girls' Catholic academy, from balloons on lockers to chipped nail polish to hair ribbons in my classmates' ponytails. But when I walked through the main entrance and saw the familiar photographs, trophies, art, and religious statues, the coincidence felt more like symbol, a tangible reminder of how this place would always be a part of me.

My decision to attend an all-girls' high school—a choice made at a time when boys were just appearing on my radar—initiated my growth into womanhood. Here I had the chance to find and nurture my voice, to take on leadership roles, and to explore my spirituality in a safe and supportive setting. I graduated with a deep sense of my inherent worth and dignity, which informs the self-assurance that carries me through life today.

My "bestest" friend walked into the reunion with me. We had met on the first day of freshman year, being the only two girls on the bus we shared with the local all boys' school, and remained close ever since, so it felt fitting we came in side by side for this milestone. One by one I said hello to my former classmates, and with each hug memories washed over me: She sat next to me in class. She was in my retreat group. She was always so kind. She and I used to be close.

The first words out of many classmates' mouths to me? "I read your blog! I see it on Facebook!" It occurred to me that maybe social media will make reunions passé, keeping us abreast in real time of the ups and downs we would otherwise digest in one lump sum every five to ten years in the school gym. I hope not. Seeing these women again reminded me that profile pictures are not the same as real-time expressions. We may not be good friends. We may not even be good enemies. But we owe it to ourselves and our shared past to acknowledge our bond.

We had arrived in packs, clustering with the friends who had visited our college apartments and stood in our weddings. But if the last 10 years have taught me anything, it's that we can't predict the trajectory of our relationships. Who from the hallways will be standing with me at the 25th reunion? The 50th? I can make a pretty good guess, but there might be a few surprises too. That in itself wouldn't surprise me. Classmates are people, and people move and stretch in directions you can't predict. Someone might not be part of my life later. Others will be part of my life always. That's the beauty of remembering and reuniting.

Reunite

God, bless the currents of people who move in and out of my life, each attuned to their own rhythms, each flowing at their own pace.

Run us perpendicular when we need each other. Run us parallel when we don't. But always keep them in my sight— and yours—if only to smile and wave hello.

Amen.

Loosen Up

Relationships—be they with you, family, friends, or partners—were never meant to be static. How could they be? Free will cuts across our lives, especially in the decisions we make and the emotions we act upon when it comes to those we love.

You who defines love, you who are Love—please help me remember who I have, who they are, and who they are not. Help them remember the same of me.

We are bound to forget and to hurt. We are bound to misstep and mistake and misspeak. But we are also bound to one another by your grace.

Loosen my grip on what I cannot control in others' decisions or responses. Tighten my ability to choose rightly and wisely in my own. May I see my relationships in spectrum. May I be dazzled by their array.

Amen.

Forgive and Remember

Withholding forgiveness requires far greater energy than granting it. You have to continue fuming, stoke the fire, fan the flames. That takes dedication and meditation, time and effort that might be better served cultivating the strength to release it.

You give us such a short span down here, God. Why waste it on stifling bitterness, regret, and recrimination when we can experience liberating grace instead?

Teach me forgiveness, gentle God. Give me equal conviction in letting go as I have in holding on. Be with me at those moments when my heart is hardening, and keep it soft with this soothing reminder: Forgiving does not mean forgetting. It means remembering whom and what I serve, which is all-consuming Love.

Amen.

Dating:

What If I Die Alone?

When the Service Has Ended

When the service has ended
And the liquor is drained
And the food's packed as leftovers
And the music's last strain
Fades into memory
Like the flavor of cake
And my buzz dissipates
Leaving blah in its wake,
The newlyweds leave me
Alone in the hall
Holding bouquets
And the thought: *Is this all*
That I'm destined for?
All that I'll earn?
All I look forward to,
All that I'll learn?
But the answers aren't there,
Just heel- and heart-sores
And petals that droop
As they drift to the floor.

Avow

What vow are you asking me to take, God?

To love and to cherish till death do us part? (Then who's the other half of "us"?)

To be obedient, chaste, and poor in religious life? (Then where's my stigmata, my proof?)

To consecrate my single status? (Then why do I feel lonely?)

Most of us have no clue how to answer that question, and in trying to answer it, we only feel more acutely what a rejoicing, sad, confusing, revelatory existence you gave us to stumble through.

Yes, you tell us your love is enough. Yes, you tell us you are the ultimate partner. But you are not mortal. You are not my community. You are not my friends. You are not my lovers.

Surely these groups are divine in their own way. Why not reveal them to me sooner—and with them, the answer to my vows?

Amen.

The Insignificant Other

In historic preservation, sites under consideration for the National Register of Historic Places must identify their period of significance, or the span of time in which whatever makes the place noteworthy occurred. It could be an event, a person, a distinctive architectural trait, or "the potential to yield important information." In the National Park Service's words (Volume 39 of its National Register Bulletin), "events and associations with historic properties are finite; most properties have a clearly definable period of significance."

People, however, are not buildings. We are far from finite (barring, of course, our earthly lifespans), and bring with us myriad ways, modes, traits, and choices that vary our significance to different people at different points in our lives. Why then do we as a society perpetuate the phrase "significant other?" If we were to apply a preservation context to this phrase, we are saying that this person (the "SO") has "a clearly definable period of significance." Yet when we use this phrase, we're usually in the midst of our time with them. We have no knowledge of how long or to what degree they will remain significant. Instead, we make a big call in real time: a risky, potentially inaccurate move.

Moreover, to call someone a significant other is to assume that we have identified what makes them noteworthy for us. In the best-case scenario, they are significant because we love them and have entered together with them into a fulfilling, meaningful relationship. In the worst-case scenario, they are significant because they have a pulse and we bring them to parties. The former is uplifting; the latter, dispiriting.

Of course, neither point matters when you consider how the very phrase negates itself. "Significant" implies that this person is worthy of attention, that they carry influence in one's life, that they have made an impression. But then we tack on "other," a xenophobic word choice that smacks of separatism and opposite-ness, alluding to a foreign object that has somehow wiggled its way into our bloodstreams and staked out parasitic ground, a stranger that gains a body only when it is part of a pair. So when we say "significant other," we're really saying "noteworthy nothing." Or, more bluntly, "insignificant."

I don't want to be considered insignificant to people I care about, nor do I want to burden insignificant interlopers with a phrase that paradoxically inflates and removes their importance. If someone's name is going to be attached to mine in conversation or on the fronts of envelopes, then I want them to be an equal, fully formed person—not a checked box, not a stroke for my ego, and certainly not a lazy, imprecise shorthand for "not single."

What am I asking for here? I want us all to acknowledge that any person, romantic or otherwise, whom we let across our welcome mats will enjoy a period of significance in our lives, and that if we've let them in that far to begin with, then they can never truly be "other" to us again.

What's more, we are far from "other" to ourselves. Regardless of what roles we inhabit in our external relationships, our relationship to ourselves is constant and the root of our sense of self-worth. Our personal periods of significance last as long as we believe them to be so, hopefully from the day we emerge to the day we croak. And when we have each deemed ourselves significant—as independent, cultivated, substantial people with "important information" always bubbling up—we will stand marked as so.

Please, let's retire "significant other." It speaks nothing to the power that true relationships hold and even less about the value we place in ourselves.

The Welcome Mat at the Castle Gates

I've laid the welcome mat outside the gates.
(My gators ate the first one, but I will
Not be deterred.) It rests there, flat and striped,
Beyond the sulfur moat that belches fumes,
Beneath the poison arrows that land true,
Beside the wobbly ladders doomed to fall,
Not far from cauldrons bloated with hot tar.
For I, with wisdom gleaned from faith alone,
Know that the person who can reach the mat
And ring the doorbell, interrupting lunch,
Deserves to join me in the peaceful courtyard,
Take the other armchair at the hearth,
And help me find rooms even I've not seen.

Amen.

Love Letter to a Break-Up (and Its Ally)

Dear Break-Up:

Time for a post-mortem (emphasis on mortem). How easy it was to stick with the status quo, even when the quo involved distance and graduate school. How tempting it was, when I lapsed into doubt, to return to the relationship résumé, the one that made us perfect together on paper, the one that argued how in today's kiss-and-run dating world we had all the ingredients for long-term success.

Break-Up, you were wily. You always skipped around the back of my mind after hard conversations. Your ears perked when warning bells chimed during everyday moments. Yet you had the absolute hubris to play devil's advocate: "Look at the values you share. That shouldn't annoy you. You need to be more understanding."

Be honest: you liked to play the fear card, too. "I don't want to hurt someone I care about. I'm afraid of having to date again. The love of novels and rom-coms doesn't exist."

Then your better half—the still, small voice—asserted herself. She'd been gently prodding me for months, you know. She sensed what lay outside my rational arguments. And she asked questions. Hard ones. Ones I plugged my ears against and cried about at night. I have journal pages packed with half-answers and half-lies, all in response to her.

She played the fear card, too, though in a different way. "I can't spend my whole life with someone who doesn't make my heart leap. I don't want a marriage that dies by death of a thousand paper cuts. I don't want to miss out on everything I am supposed to become."

When the internal dialogue reached the breaking point, she stepped out from her shadowy corner and took my hand.

"Do you trust me?" she asked.

"Not really," I said.

"Can you try?" she asked.

"Do I have a choice?" I replied.

"Not really," she shrugged. "But don't worry. I've got you."

Then you swooped in for the kill, Break-Up. Together, we three did the deed.

I say to people now, "I'm the one who initiated it." But I know that you know that we both know someone else did. It's whoever owns the still, small voice in my gut. It's the kind but persistent nag. She did it.

Thanks to the two of you, I'm back to wondering what and whom I'm meant for. Unlike past forays into lovelorn daydreams, though, I have new fortifications. For example, I'm recommitted to what love means for and to me. I accept that ending a relationship, especially the un-right ones, counts as success, not failure. I'm tuning out my uterus and thinking of my soul.

For all this I thank you, Break-Up—and even bigger thanks to your better half. Despite my grousing, I appreciate your efforts now, and will probably appreciate them even more in the future.

Take care (of me and others)—

Me

Catch Me If I Let You

You prompt, you cajole, you urge me to jump . . . yet you don't present the net. Fair? I think not.

Sorry, I'm not giving you the satisfaction of my abject fear and terror. I'm staying right here on my ledge. I have a pillow and some snacks. I'm good to go. You'll just have to sit there, somewhere below me in the mist, holding a net (allegedly), waiting. I hope you brought water, because this could take a while.

I'm fine with talking while we sit here. We can talk the whole damn day. Why don't we talk about the fact you want me to pitch forward on a mere whim, with the vague reassurance of "it'll be okay" as my parachute?

No, I'm not misunderstanding the situation. You want me to JUMP. Laws of gravity dictate that I will plummet once my feet leave this ledge. I will fall down. Most likely in a hard and splattering fashion.

Well, have you ever seen anybody fall up?

Really?

So gravity doesn't apply? I just jump, stretch out my arms, and grab you?

Hmm. That does remove the need for a net I can't see. Though I'm struggling with the whole "lack of gravity and other natural laws" part of this idea . . .

Let me think about it, ok? This is a rather different proposition. I need to mull it over. And eat some snacks.

But I do hear you. Stay close by; we'll keep talking. That will help. Thanks. Want a Cheez-It?

Amen.

The Break-Up: A Sonnet

You are not right for me. So there. It's said.
I could keep up charades, but we both know
The longer that I try to force a glow,
The closer we'll both be to being dead—
Which means less time (I say with creeping dread)
For each of us to wander high and low
And—finding Cupid—jump him for his bow
To arrow whom we're meant to love instead.

But then I peer into the yawning hole
Where plus-ones disappear—negated, lost—
And all my heart's investments sink to naught:
No ring, no home, no child, no mated soul.
I'm tempted thus to disregard the cost
Of speaking less than truth, even if fraught.

For Anyone Who's Ever Broken Up with Someone Else

To my God
who speaks to me with a still, small voice
who helps me hold up my end of the bargain
who governs all love, be it lost, found, or yet unknown—

I ask you
to forgive me for hurting another person
to hug me tight as I relive every prior break-up through the
lens of the latest
to help me resist the temptation to seek comfort from the one
other person I know is grieving the same loss I am
to give me the courage to keep seeking

to keep hoping
to keep trusting
to keep loving

and to pray the prayer I feel selfish praying
but which is not selfish at all
because you have placed it in my heart.

Amen.

Better Half

All great partnerships

begin with trust
deepen with compromise
evolve with sacrifice
expand with revelation

yet never burst their bindings

for love
and friendship
and respect
are most forgiving knots.

Help me tie them tight, God. Help me be a better half.

Amen.

Falling for You

God of hand-holding and hand-wringing,

Cradle me as I figure out how to be present to myself as well as to those I love. Let me peek through your fingers and spot when my people are striving to give to me as I am striving to give to them. Caress me when I am anxious; block me when I am injurious. And if you must let me go, let it be so I may continue falling in love—with him, with her, with them, with myself—all intoxicating reflections of you.

Amen.

Commitment:

Why Is Falling in Love So Terrifying?

An Open Letter to the Love of My Life (I)

Dear love of my life,

I think of you when I'm cooking dinner. When I'm running errands. When I'm wearing sweatpants. When I'm feeling attractive. I think of you in all the small, in-between moments that comprise 90 percent of our lives, yet are much more noticed when you have someone noticing them with you.

I think of you at the holidays, too. At weddings. At funerals. At births. I think of you in all the moving, seismic shifts that comprise 10 percent of our lives yet feel close to its entirety because these shifts remind us why we're alive and that we're living them together.

I think of our kids, our vacations, our dates, our fights, our accumulated history that as of today has yet to start accumulating. I think of all we will share, and I'm impatient, because I know we're going to be awesome and I want the awesome to start RIGHT. NOW.

I don't think of your face. There are 7 billion people in the world. You will look like a combination of two of them. That's all I know.

I do think of your heart and mind a lot, though. Don't ask me how, but I just know, somewhere in my heart, how they look. They are bright. Kind. Compassionate. Feeling. Loving. Funny. Adventurous. Thoughtful. Good.

Good.

That's the conviction I summon when couples walk by me in the busy city and their locked hands pack a double fist to my chest. That's the assurance I cling to when I see two people blossom into their ripest, most loving selves with each other. I know that you are good, and that you are out there, and that you are waiting.

Yet it's bigger than waiting. Just like me, you're preparing. You're out there with your friends, your family, your job, your life. You're cooking dinner, running errands, attending weddings and funerals, visiting your family. You're watching others pair up. You're wondering who is out there for you. And every triumph and tragedy—every moment when you're lonely, confused, content, or overjoyed—is molding you into the person who will want me.

Who are you? Where are you? When are you? The questions roll around in my mind. I know better than to expect the answers in a given timeframe. It doesn't keep me from asking, but really, I do know the answers will come in due time. Or, at least, I hope—trust—they will.

Until then . . . expect and demand the best. Of yourself, of me, of us. Prepare for imperfection from all sides. Stock up on sticky notes to leave around the house for me. Get excited. And be good, ok?

Love,
Me

Open Prayer, Part 1

Hey you. Yes, you. I can't wait to meet you.

Please exist. Please hurry up. Because once we meet, the rest will all make sense.

Amen.

An Open Letter to the Love of My Life (II)

Dear love of my life,

Hi again. I wrote to you about a month ago—did you reply? I haven't gotten a signed letter or a call from a number identified as "LOVE OF YOUR LIFE" on my phone, so I can't be sure.

Once, when I was debating whether I should end a previous relationship, my patient spiritual director let me moan and groan and snot for a good 10 minutes and then asked, quite simply: "Are you crazy about him?"

I couldn't answer her out loud. Because I knew if my boyfriend and I had the kind of love that would see us through to the bitter, sweet, complex end, the answer should be yes. But I couldn't say yes. So I didn't say anything.

There was my answer. To everything.

That's what it's going to come down to in the end. You and I are going to be wild about each other. We're going to crack each other up, go on play dates well into our 90s, tease our kids mercilessly, hold hands at the grocery store, attempt to eat healthily but always resort to ice cream, look around rooms to see if the other has come in yet.

You'll be crazy about me. I'll be crazy about you. No big questions. No big doubts. Just calm assurance from the still, small voice.

In the meantime, I am descending into a pit of emotional wackiness and overblown chocolate consumption. Feel free to get in touch soon. We could all use a break.

Love,

Me

Open Prayer, Part 2

I will tell you you're the best.

I will also apologize when my dog chews your shoes, gnaws your clothes, and steals your food. I know this will happen because no matter how old my dog is when I meet you, he will still be eating things he shouldn't be eating.

I look forward to thanking you for the chocolate cake you'll bring home for every occasion, because you will know me well enough to know that I love chocolate cake about as much as you, and you'll be fine with that. (I'd also like to thank you in advance for sharing the last cookie with me.)

Be warned: I probably won't know at first how to love you the way that you want, need, or deserve. But I will do everything I can to learn. For you, I will never stop learning how to love better. And I know that you will do the same for me.

Love is a decision. Love will be found. And hopefully found again, and again, and again, all with the same person. Because I love the idea of rediscovery—even if I did learn it from Journey's "Faithfully."

Amen.

An Open Letter to the Love of My Life (III)

Howdy love,

Happy Valentine's Day, wherever/whoever you are! Perhaps you're expecting me to rag about the holiday? This might come as a surprise given my current relationship status, but I don't actually hate V-Day. Its over-commercialization and ooey-gooey sentiment? Yes, I hate that. The bitter "Single's Awareness Day" anti-Valentine snark? Yes, I hate that too. But the idea of a day devoted to love? What's not to love about that?

Amid the blaring red hearts and sappy songs, I've been thinking about the core of love—its mystery, its awe, its demands. I've been thinking about my family, my friends, my colleagues, my fellow movers-about-the-world, my God. I love them all in their own way, some more easily, some more deeply than others.

Here's the sticky wicket about love, though: if you're truly open to it, you risk becoming unmoored. I think that's the truer meaning of "swept off your feet"—that you've left yourself so vulnerable to this remarkable emotion that you relinquish control and go off in the tide. When I write that out, the idea frightens me. But it entices me as well. I want more of that powerful sweep in my life—with God, with family, with friends, with you.

In the absence of a V-Day date, I'm going to make you a promise. Promises, after all, are commitments. IOUs, if you will. And I'm committed if nothing else.

I promise to be open to love. Not just love of you, but all love. Real love. Love at its core. I promise to invite, seek, and appreciate it. I promise to form it where it doesn't exist. For I believe that knowing love—*living* love—will lead me to everything that's worth having in this world.

Love,
Me

Open Prayer, Part 3

I promise to reach for your hand (and your butt) 5, 20, 68 years in.

I promise to grow comfortable with you without taking you for granted.

I promise to enjoy and acknowledge our love and to be responsive to its needs, as if it were a living thing to be tended.

I promise that even if all the other parts in my life fall through, nothing will give me greater joy than keeping these promises to you.

Amen.

The Best We Can

God of partnership,

Help the just-because flowers grow
and the love note ink flow
and the broken record show

that we're doing the best we can by each other
in earnest imitation
of you.

Amen.

How Jane Eyre Saved My Relationship

Do you think I can stay to become nothing to you? Do you think I am an automaton?—a machine without feelings? and can bear to have my morsel of bread snatched from my lips, and my drop of living water dashed from my cup? Do you think, because I am poor, obscure, plain, and little, I am soulless and heartless? You think wrong!—I have as much soul as you,—and full as much heart! And if God had gifted me with some beauty and much wealth, I should have made it as hard for you to leave me, as it is now for me to leave you. I am not talking to you now through the medium of custom, conventionalities, nor even of mortal flesh;—it is my spirit that addresses your spirit; just as if both had passed through the grave, and we stood at God's feet, equal,—as we are!

—Charlotte Bronte, *Jane Eyre*

Potential title of this essay: How Jane Eyre *ruined* my relationship.

I never thought I'd say something like that. I've read the book at least a dozen times and become an expert in all filmed representations of Mr. Rochester. (Best physical casting: Ciaran Hinds version. Best screenplay adaptation: Toby Stephens version. Best use of Michael Fassbender in tight white pants: Michael Fassbender version.) Since my awkward teenage years, Jane Eyre and Mr. Rochester have been my shining beacon of hope from Relationship Hill. Whenever I feel sentimental, despondent, or at loose ends, I turn to them. I love that Jane, despite her youth, balances vulnerability, self-knowledge, and conviction with poise and grace, and I love that Rochester, despite his inner demons, maintains a sense of humor, a wonder for love, and an intense desire to live with joy.

So how, you ask, could such beloved characters possibly turn me against love? Well, they didn't do anything; I did. Namely, I got older and entered real-life adult relationships with plenty of ups and downs. And in one instance of a very down down—a pivotal moment where I was seriously questioning if my partner and I were putting anywhere near equal amounts of effort into maintaining a long-distance relationship—I asked myself a fundamental question: Do I love him enough to continue?

The gravity of the question demanded a dose of Jane, so I popped in one of the movie versions, settled on the couch, and instantly felt terrible. There were Jane and Rochester, parading around on the screen, full of love and intensity and witty repartee. There they were with pronouncements of affection and can't-live-without-yous. There they were kissing in the rain, stealing glances, running into each other's arms. There they were making me want to vomit because I had zero of that in my life. I spent the first half of the film teary and hiccupping, convinced that true love was all raindrops and banter and declarations, and that I was doomed to never have it.

By the second half, however, I was remembering the less rosy elements of the storyline. Rochester flat-out lied to Jane about his marital status. Jane was naive and inexperienced with the wider world. They broke each other's hearts and miscommunicated and suffered a hard, jagged, abrupt split when Jane ran away to the moors, intending never to return.

Ah, the moors. When I was younger, this was my least favorite part of the story—slow, tedious, and preachy. But as I get older, I appreciate how much happens with Jane while she's there. For example, she contributes to her little community by starting a girls' school. She makes friends for the first time since childhood. She discovers relatives she never knew she had but always wanted. She rejects a marriage proposal (a huge risk for a woman in her era) because she's not in love with the man. And in the ultimate payoff from the narrative universe, she comes into some money, guaranteeing her freedom.

When Jane returns to Rochester after her moor adventure, it's as a well-rounded woman who tested her principles and convictions in the real world and found them up to the task. She comes back to Rochester because she forgives him, because she knows what they are capable of together, because she chooses to. Meanwhile, Rochester—whose estate fire has stripped his wealth, taken his sight, and removed his first wife from the scene—welcomes Jane back as an unfettered man. He responds not to her looks, but to her spirit. He acts with more honesty and humility. He chooses to move forward with her.

That's when I saw it: this was my relationship's moment on the moors. Our moment to examine if the foundation was strong, even if the house was ablaze. Our moment to accept that love is not perfect roses and sunshine, but an active choice—one we both must make.

Jane and Rochester are adults. They acknowledge their flaws, ask forgiveness, and strive to improve. They are perfect together in their imperfection. We root for them not because they mystically hear each other's voices in the wind (not my favorite part of the book), but because 99 percent of the time they are struggling, making mistakes, and trying their best to follow their hearts.

Once the movie ended, I ejected the DVD and called my partner to talk. We took some time to think. We talked again. We felt better. The very down down started to look up again.

When it comes to relationships, we don't need Gothic narratives. Life is dramatic enough. Still, Jane and Rochester are my standard bearers—proof that for the right people, moors are not a death knell, but an opportunity.

"We Stood at God's Feet, Equal"

When the ratio of daydreams to sleepless nights tilts right,
When inside jokes drop off and outside fears creep in,
When ears no longer hear over sniping heart and mind—

Restore the balance between us, reveal what we are made of, and remind us we're not alone on this quest to love.

Amen.

Engaged!

> There was an intense emotionality at this time: music I
> loved, or the long golden sunlight of late afternoon, would
> set me weeping. I was not sure what I was weeping for, but
> I would feel an intense sense of love, death, and transience,
> inseparably mixed.
>
> —Oliver Sacks, *On the Move*

So much I want to say, and no clue where to begin.

I could start with the moment he proposed to me beside an
outcrop of rocks near the Sky Meadows trailhead, but that
moment was surreal.

I could start with the thrilled, marveling look on his face
(mirrored on mine) when we first used the word fiancé, but that
look was fleeting.

I could start with the unnerving sensation of my feet floating three feet above the ground, levitated by the outpouring of
love and support and exclamation from the people dearest to
us, but that sensation moves me to tears every time I examine
it, and writing an entire essay about it might lead to
hospitalization.

Instead I will start with my first lesson of engaged life: that
to be on the other side of engagement is to learn exactly what
it entails and why it is, in fact, a really big deal.

I don't say that last statement tongue in cheek. After all, I
am part of a faith tradition that celebrates marriage, and I have
always applauded sincere commitment, the sacrifice and "death
to self" that it entails. It's more that my fiancé (!!) and I had
been saying to each other for months that we were "engaged in
our hearts," so what, we thought, could a mere question and
answer change?

Apparently, everything.

Stating our commitment out loud—officially, formally, in a
way that asks everyone in our lives to bear witness and keep us
accountable—kicked the whole endeavor up six notches. We

told the world we were serious about each other and our shared life, and by gum, the world was going to hold us to it.

And that was just the external effect. An internal shift would happen too that I didn't fully grasp until my now-fiancé was standing before me, sharing how much he loved me and holding an oval box in his hand. Suddenly after years of faceless, backdrop-less daydreams about my future partner, it hit me: Here was the real person, the real deal, and the reality was a million times more profound than anything I'd ever imagined on my own. (Which is saying something, because I have a very active imagination.) I finally grasped the full measure and value of my past experiences and relationships, however confused or painful or breathtaking they were. I would not have become who I was, nor so fully appreciated my partner, without them. How healing it was, then, to have found my person. How healing to love him. How healing to experience his love in return.

So much I want to say and no clue how to say it. Instead I will simply say: he is here. The bright, kind, compassionate, loving, funny, adventurous, thoughtful, good person I always envisioned. He is finally, beautifully here. He is standing before me. He is standing beside me. He wants me as much as I want him. We are creating a future together, a terrific marriage, one that, God willing, will involve board game nights and Pizza Fridays and bocce on the back lawn and a thriving kitchen garden and Post-It love notes and trips around the world and fat babies we will squeeze and love until they grow up and maybe have fat babies of their own whom we'll squeeze and love, and all because we had the great good fortune to join the same guitar group at church, strike up a conversation, and fall in love.

So much I want to say, but now I have a lifetime to say it to him, over and over and over again.

That's where we'll begin, then. With love.

Covenant

God of loving covenants,

Be the hand that underwrites our contract. Be the witness to our pledge and the buttress for our vows. Help us keep our soul-deep promise to each other as we prepare our own covenant—one that honors capital-L LOVE, which is to say, you.

Thank you for the opportunity to love someone deeply and completely. My puny human heart is blossoming ten-fold in gratitude's bright light.

Amen.

Leap of Faith

Be with us as we leave the plane, pull the cord, and hurtle headlong into the rest of our lives. Make our descent productive and our landing soft, and when we have stopped bouncing, let us help each other to our feet and revel in the brave new world we get to build together.

Amen.

On the Eve of My Wedding

As if drawn by magnets, I have ended up behind, near, or next
to the same couple at church every weekend for the past month.
They are later-middle-aged. Both are overweight. The wife uses
a cane for her pronounced limp. The husband is losing his hair.
Always, always, they are touching.

His hand never leaves her—her arm, her waist, her back.
She leans her head on his shoulder. They hold hands during the
homily. They caress each other in that deliberate way that bears
the hallmark of conscious, intentional connection. In sickness
and in health, in good times and bad, they hold each other—not
as a drowning person grips a preserver, but as a parent holds a
newborn, with quiet, protective confidence.

Even three pews back, I feel their warmth. They look at each
other's aging, asymmetrical faces with the kind of joyful gaze
that makes the object in its sights immortal and invincible.

Tonight, on the eve of our wedding, I pray that my spouse-
to-be and I become this couple. May we become this way to
each other. May we become love.

Beyond Words

This is serious, God. This is real. This is raw and daunting and profound. This moment evokes mortality alongside meaning, sacrifice alongside choice. Our vows are not lines to mumble; they are promises to solemnify.

Tonight I feel the gravity of that solemnity, the heft of the rest of our lives. We are not sentimental about this moment, God. Marriage will take us to our graves. It will wear us down, wring us dry, ask everything we have, and we are pretty much guaranteed to stumble because we are imperfect, imprecise humans.

But we will succeed where it matters most, God. We will keep the promise to practice love with each other, so in loving and trying and failing and loving still, we will learn what it means to love you.

Amen.

Nothing Is at Hand

Today I sliced not one, but two fingers with our new kitchen knife. Serves me right; I was using the wrong blade for the task at hand—a long vegetable slicer to chop basil—and the knife insisted on slipping gently to the left twice in a row, as if to call attention to my rookie error.

The cuts are not deep. They drew no blood, just nicked my nails and created two tiny, jagged edges that I did not have time to file before I left for my writing session, so now when I rub my fingers absentmindedly at the keyboard, I am reminded of my missteps.

Such is my life these days: a brisk march—or should I say aimless ramble?—of inefficiency that finds my muscle memory out of date, my judgment delayed, and my mental to-do lists under constant threat of scattering. I no longer feel like the reliable and punctual person I have always prided myself on being, and to tell the truth, it's making me anxious.

I could cut myself some slack, I suppose. In the last six weeks, I moved my house, moved my desk, threw a wedding, and prepared for our first international trip as a couple. But I don't cut myself much slack. I'm Type A, a top producer. I can't let incidentals like Washington, D.C. Metro track work or stifling heat waves or fruit fly upticks stand in my way. I am a doer, dammit, and doers DO, in time and on time.

One layer of what's bothering me boils down to logistics. I've had to re-plan all my public transit routes, for example, which in turn affects my once-precise, now-unpredictable time estimates. My internal meal-planning calculator has not yet readjusted for another mouth who may or may not remember to bring his lunch. Morning wakeup calls and bedtime rituals have taken on a "come what may" quality. As long as they eventually occur and we don't miss important meetings, we consider them a success.

Ah, there's that "we"—the indicator of the deeper layer that's really at work in my current unsettled state. At the heart of it, I have been thrown off course by the simple fact of having another person in my daily life. Up until six weeks ago, he was a very pleasant and deftly managed visitor within my carefully calibrated routine; now he has become a still pleasant but variable constant, one with different alarms and hours and habits and, well, everything.

What I professed to know intellectually about the transition to married life is now hitting me with full emotional honesty: I am on a learning curve. A steep one. It encompasses learning about myself, about my spouse, about the routines and habits that constitute not just my life, but also the perception of my life that I've held since going off to college. I am realizing how truly convicted I am in the "rightness" of my ways. Surely no other technique can be as efficient or productive. Surely my methods do not require evolution. Surely if I keep hacking at the basil with the wrong knife, the knife will eventually see the wisdom of my approach and fall into line rather than into my fingers. Right? Isn't that how this works?

Oh no. I have brought a vegetable slicer to a gunfight.

The gun deserves to win, though. My routines are important; they make me healthy, calm, productive; but so are the shared routines under development. What we create together will find a way to balance our individual needs with our unified ones. Besides, six weeks is nothing in the grand arc of our life together. We have time. Now I will add patience.

Misplaced Mise en Place

I'm left of where I was.

I see where I used to sit, reliably within reach for all who needed me, but my recent move down the countertop has shifted my perspective. Where once I jumped into action, ready and sure, now I await rediscovery, shy and uncertain. Every meal feels off. Or maybe I'm the only thing that's changed?

Domestic God of hearth and heart—rearrange my shelves, scatter my habits, but please, when the dust settles and I have remembered to wipe it up, reveal to me who I've become.

Amen.

Accept the Sandwich

"Do you want a pork sandwich?"

I paused in my frantic packing and last-minute to-doing. My cross-country flight was in two hours. The drive to the airport would take one. By my standards we were late, and the lateness was all I could focus on, yet here was my husband asking me if I wanted a roast pork-and-peppers sandwich for the trip.

"I can make one for you right now," he said. "It's no trouble."

"No, don't worry about it, I'll do it myself in a few minutes."

He regarded me standing in the hallway, caught between rooms and tasks, and blinked. Without saying more, he went downstairs. Relieved to be left alone, I resumed my rush.

Ten minutes later I barreled down the steps. "Remember to bring the CSA bag with you on Wednesday! Would you mind changing the sheets while I'm gone? I still have to pick up the cards . . ." I ran into the kitchen. There he was with car keys in one hand and a beautiful bagged homemade sandwich ready to go, along with two granola bars and an apple.

I exhaled. Said thank you. Put the food in my carry-on. Enjoyed it on the flight. And thought with each chew how different life is when you don't have to do it all yourself.

The path to sandwich acceptance has been winding for me. Part of it has to do with ceding control, but a bigger part has to do with allowing my partner to serve me. What I perceive as extra work is for him an act of service, done out of love and care. (And maybe a will to avoid the formidable and legendary "hangry" version of me.) His gesture had nothing to do with the sandwich and everything to do with partnership.

We have a lifetime to perfect offering and accepting the sandwich. May the journey always be so delicious.

Love is Not a Condiment

Love is not a condiment. It is not separate or extra or packable or pocketable. It is not added later at one's own discretion. It is not left on the table to grow stale or sticky. It does not expire, and it cannot be sold.

Love, rather, is the main course. It's baked in, inseparable from the meal. Your server brings it to you sometimes with intention, other times by accident, but it always arrives nonetheless. At your favorite places, love is "the usual"—no order necessary.

Love is what sustains you, long after you've finished.

Amen.

How to Stay Married, According to My Parents

My parents have been married for more than forty years. For those of you who don't know my parents, this factoid might not interest you. But it should, because my parents provide an excellent example of what real marriage looks like.

With each year that passes in my own marriage, I consider anew how I perceive my parents' relationship, how it has affected my life, and what lessons I can take from them. For example, my adult eyes now recognize them as two loving, imperfect people in a loving, imperfect union. I grew up enveloped by their evident, mutual love and affection and occasionally experienced less pretty, more stressful moments too. Through it all, though, I absorbed that love deserves displaying, affection requires sharing, words are worth saying, forgiveness demands granting, and date nights need calendaring—all because my parents lived their marriage out in the open. My brother and I witnessed tickles at the sink, strained conversations, cuddling on the couch, moments of panic, love notes on scrap paper, bad days, good days, blah days, extraordinary days: the million points of minutiae that comprise a life lived together.

But for all the critical lessons and important observations, it seems that a good marriage—according to my parents, anyway—can be boiled down to six tenets:

I love you.
I want you.
I like you.
You're funny.
We did it!
Let's keep going.

Every day of marriage brings an opportunity to exercise at least one of these tenets, and on some extraordinary days, all six. For me, those days are the best days—the ones that spark memories of my parents' relationship and invite me to revel in my own.

Let's Build a Life

Let's build a life, one story at a time.

One inside joke, one special date, one memory at a time.

One fight, one makeup, one crying jag, one sidesplitter, one lesson at a time.

One table, one couch, one move, one home, one animal, one child, one stage at a time.

One card, one heartache, one surprise, one load, one list, one Monday, one meal, one morning, one moment at a time.

Let's build a life, one story at a time, and let's tell it like we mean it.

Amen.

FIVE

Why Am I Grieving?

Mortality:
Why Must We Die?

Elegy

My high school homeroom teacher will never know I associate her with skinned cats.

Mrs. Roman was one of our school's biology teachers. She was best known for her friendly and calm demeanor, relative youth (only 10 years older than us students), and her big physiology class final, which was to dissect a cat. That meant at least two days every year I'd walk into homeroom and get hit with the stench of formaldehyde—my cue to keep my eyes facing front to avoid seeing the former felines spread out across the lab tables.

Mrs. Roman will never know I associate her with skinned cats because I no longer have the opportunity to tell her. In a tragic example of life's injustice, she succumbed to cancer at 35, leaving behind a husband, three young children, and a grieving community.

Today I'm older than she was when she died, a simple chronological fact that adds a new dimension to my sorrow. Now more than a decade out from her death, I grieve for our shared past, years that keep receding further into memory, years neither of us will see again. I grieve for her children, who lose her anew at each milestone in their lives. I grieve for the opportunities we all miss to celebrate life as we're living it.

Unlike with the cats in her classroom, I cannot avoid acknowledging Mrs. Roman's death, nor any human's death. I cannot hold my breath or avert my eyes. And I'm wondering now if I should take the opportunity, even if it's only through memory and imagination, to swallow my disgust and look at the lab cats straight on. What might I learn if I observe their puckered skin and neat incisions more closely? If I allow the visceral reminder of death to recall to me my own mortality? If I resist the urge to keep loss—and fear of loss—at arm's length?

In this scenario, the Mrs. Roman I remember is sitting at her desk in front of the classroom, patient and smiling, ready to explain matters of science and sit with questions of faith. The best teachers are the ones who guide you through the unknown and await your discovery. I wonder what I will learn when I reach her again.

Carpe Vitam

To the God who exists outside of time—

In the fullness of your grace, help us forget the steady march of days and instead live in the sacred, eternal now.

You are the promise that our lives will change—not end— with death.

Amen.

On the Clothesline

When I contemplate nothingness, I experience a paradoxical rush of abandon and abandonment, a sense of being wrung out and draped over the clothesline yet not pinned firmly enough to avoid being carried away on a stiff breeze.

The prevailing winds will catch me with or without my consent, so I'd prefer to leave with grace and dignity intact, perhaps even with a spirit of adventure. But I'm not there yet. Lend me clothespins—two or three should do the trick—to keep me feeling connected until I'm released from the line.

Amen.

Just Beyond

I can't conceive of nothing while I'm something.
I can't imagine being blank, being non,
Being anything but what you made me now.

Yet with her obit tacked up on the fridge—
A life compressed to less than 80 words—
I have to face my own mortality,
And the thought of leaving all I've ever known
Is cause enough to hyperventilate.

God, you promise us a great beyond
In every sense—beyond our limbs and skin,
Beyond our earth, beyond our comprehension.

It seems too good, too perfect, to be true.
Cheat death and pain, yet live in constant joy?
Such magnitude of hope is staggering.

Mind you, I don't want to discover if
You're right for many decades yet to come.
But I would not mind following that hope
And finding where it leads.

That seems the best.
For now.
At least tonight, as I drift off . . .

Amen.

The Procession of Grief

In an era of GPS, Google maps, and smartphones, why do we still have funeral processions?

I asked myself this on a frigid Friday one February as I impatiently tapped the gas pedal of my rental car, stuck in the middle of a long row of vehicle-bound mourners for a dear family friend. My four-ways were flashing; the procession tag was stuck in my dash; my youngest cousin was seated beside me. Our route was set to go through neighborhoods in and around the area where I grew up, places I hadn't considered in decades, much less seen. "It should take 45 minutes," the funeral director said through my passenger window.

The line began to move. I followed suit. Within a few minutes I saw that this endeavor was going to result in gray hair or a totaled car. No matter how closely I paid attention or drew Lamaze-like breaths, I could not get into the flow. The idea of blowing through red lights scraped against every defensive driving instinct I've ever built up. I either hit the brakes too hard, bouncing my petite cousin against her seatbelt, or left too much room between cars, allowing non-mourners to break our chain. The result was a herky-jerky, brake-or-bust stumble through the outskirts of Philadelphia—a display so inept that my parents called me from their car, one ahead, to reiterate the rules of procession.

By the time we arrived at the cemetery, I was stressed and sweating. My poor cousin was an unsavory shade of chartreuse. We both leaped from the car the minute I put it in park, not considering how it appeared to look so over-eager at a graveside. But we made it there. Together. Even though I'd almost rear-ended my own parents at several points, they were now standing with me and dozens of other mourners, united in mourning and remembrance for someone we loved.

Removed from the car, now able to view it at a safe, still distance, I recognized the funeral procession as the vehicular manifestation of grief and consolation. When you are part of a procession, you are not just driving a route; you are entering a long continuum of suffering that incorporates your personal experience and winds back through that of every other human who has followed a body to its inevitable final stop. You are moving with others who share your emotions while allowing people outside your bubble to sacrifice a few moments of their day to make your way a little easier at a difficult time.

My defensive driving, it turns out, was too defensive. I was trying too hard to control a process that, to be most effective, required me to let go. I should have instead relaxed into the grief, allowed the current to carry me to the cemetery, to our loved one's side one last time.

The minute the final rites ended, my cousin escaped to her family's car, and my mother joined me in the rental. As the cars passed the cemetery gate and hit the main road, they scattered, charting their own routes to the hall for the luncheon. With no procession to lead us back, I fired up the GPS. I followed the automated voice's instructions. I obeyed traffic signals. More calm and predictable, yes. But also bereft—a solitary car on a solitary journey, yearning for community.

Graveyard

Each day we have a funeral. We die a little, cry a bit, bury something, and leave our woes and frustrations and expectations in hidden mounds throughout our existence.

But out of sight is not out of mind. These personal graveyards are fresh earth. They give way beneath our feet. They remind us we are flawed and fleeting.

What would happen if we didn't try to bury our imperfections but embraced them? Didn't hide them in shame but released them? Then the ground would be unbroken, and wisdom from the deed—rather than knowledge of where we hid the bodies—would guide us. We wouldn't perish, but simply let go.

God of the living, uncover all the little gravesites of my life. Exhume the weary ghosts and let them float up and away, drawing my gaze toward you.

Amen.

Share the Lasagna: A Useful Lesson for Co-Grievers

When tragedy befalls people I love, I wonder if my actions are enough. Should I call? Send flowers? Donate? Fly out to the funeral? Give them space? Bake eight lasagnas, put six in their freezers, and eat two myself?

In these moments I think about my experience with one of my oldest friends who first lost her father and then two years later her mother, both to cancer. I was with my friend in the days immediately following her mother's death as she arranged the funeral and welcomed visitors to the house. We looked through photo albums together and shared memories at the dinner table. We wallowed in occasional gallows humor. There was a lot of hugging. A lot of crying. A lot of listening. A lot of wordlessness, not because we ran out of things to say, but because what we wanted to discuss was beyond conversation.

In the midst of that long weekend, a package arrived for my friend. Another friend in a different state, anxious that my friend hadn't been able to pack enough clothes for her now-extended stay, bought and mailed several casual outfits "just in case." My friend cried when she opened the package. I did, too—mainly because I feared I would never be so proactive for someone I loved.

When it comes to supporting loved ones through grief, is doing nothing better than doing the wrong thing? Does "the wrong thing" even exist in such extraordinary circumstances? Sure, I would probably never think to send clothes to a friend. But listening, sending cards, and making food are perfectly acceptable because they are what *I* can offer. And meanwhile, other friends and family are offering what they can. At any given moment someone will step up for their loved one. Our collective force, these intricate and emotional human webs, is catching and bearing the people who need it. It doesn't relieve us of individual responsibility, but it does relieve us of the pressure to be everything.

So this is what I take forward now in times of grief: Be present. Act in thoughtful love. Share the lasagna.

To the Griever, From Your Co-Griever

I called because I missed you and wanted to hear your voice.

I hugged you because, for weeks, I couldn't and wanted to be sure you were really here.

I joked with you because I have the brain space to see right now that life is still funny and wanted you to see it, too.

I cried with you because I ran out of words.

I am selfish and nosy and pushy, probably full of fixes you don't want and solutions you can't have. But if I do manage to hit on what you need—the exact right thing at the exact right moment—then grab it with both hands and don't let go. Be selfish, nosy, and pushy right back. That's where we'll meet in the middle, and that's how we'll pull through this. Together.

Amen.

When Heaven Is Wedded to Earth

Night truly blessed
when heaven is wedded to earth
and man is reconciled with God!
                    —Easter Vigil Proclamation

[T]here was a raised stone dais in the center of the lowered
floor, and upon this dais stood a stone archway that looked
so ancient, cracked, and crumbling that Harry was amazed
the thing was still standing. Unsupported by the surrounding
wall, the archway was hung with a tattered black curtain or
veil which, despite the complete stillness of the cold
surrounding air, was fluttering very slightly as though it had
been touched . . .

He had the strangest feeling that there was someone
standing right behind the veil on the other side of the
archway. Gripping his wand very tightly, he edged around
the dais, but there was nobody there. All that could be seen
was the other side of the tattered black veil . . .

Harry thought the archway had a kind of beauty about it,
old though it was. . . . But he did not move. He had just
heard something. There were faint whispering, murmuring
noises coming from the other side of the veil.
                    —J.K. Rowling, *Harry Potter and the Order
                    of the Phoenix*

Christmas is a cakewalk for Christians, belief-wise. It's about
life, hope, new babies, tinsel. Easter, on the other hand, is
provocative. It asks us to confront death, then believe in eternal
life. To appreciate the full religious implications of the Easter
feast, I must first acknowledge sin, pain, suffering, and mortality. (Is this why we started leaving Easter baskets of chocolate?
For self-soothing?)

Despite the spiritual rewards, Easter can be a tough road to
walk each year. One Lent I had a particularly vivid reminder of

death. My maternal grandfather—a hearty *paisano* who at
90 years old was still doing his own house- and yard-work—
passed away after a month of illness. It was really the only
month in his life he was seriously sick.

He died peacefully during Holy Week with my grandmother
at his side, surrounded by family. We celebrated his life the day
after Easter. I helped cantor the funeral mass. At the cemetery
an Honor Guard folded the flag and played taps, and the whole
clan watched the workers seal the burial plot. Afterward my
grandmother clasped her hands and exclaimed, "With a service
like that, who can be sad?"

Her sentiment was sincere and Easter-y, one I agreed with
in principle but wasn't exactly feeling. My grandfather's swift
decline had reawakened all my anxieties about the reality of
death, the nature of the afterlife, the weight of eternity, and the
meaning of life on earth. I was trying to simultaneously experience and contemplate grief, but I wasn't having much success. I
was a full-on emotional ninny.

Then I remembered a conversation from the day before.
While on a walk, my mom and I had talked about the morning
Grandpop died. "You know, when I was at the hospital with the
body, I turned to my sister and said, 'I'm jealous,'" my mother
told me. "What does he know now that we don't know?" She
paused. "What does it say about the human condition that we
work so hard to figure out what comes next? That we actually
try to study this? We're never going to figure it out. The only
way to know is to die. Period."

I understood her point. But I also think we have many ways
"to die." We can keel over. Expire. Give in. Sacrifice. Let go.
Accept. Dying in all its forms, physical and spiritual, shortens
the distance between our human existence and the great
unknown. It draws us closer to the veil—so close that we might
feel it flutter, and we might hear voices, even if we won't get to
see through it until the last step.

Once I was back in my own house and routine, away from
the viewing, funeral, and endless deli platters, I heard Grandpop's

voice. He called me with his Philly accent—"Jewlya!"—and I fell into a memory:

I'm eight years old. The days are getting longer. The school year is waning. Grandmom is cooking dinner up at the house, but I'm with Grandpop in his tomato beds at the foot of the steep hill in their backyard. The air is pungent and green. Grandpop moves gingerly through the rows, checking his bumper crop. His workman hands—the ones that fix motors and light Marlboro Reds—are gentle with the new fruit. He points out the yellow flowers where new tomatoes will grow. The huge trees overhead dapple the setting sun as we pick a couple good ones for dinner. The stems are prickly. Mulch gets stuck in my shoelaces. And that green smell, the smell of a garden at work, the smell of sweat and white cotton T-shirts, the smell of love in the soil, is ever-present.

At that quiet moment in the past, heaven was wedded to earth, and I didn't know it. I didn't mark it with words or ceremony. I didn't take a picture. I didn't need to. I was living the blessing with someone I loved. Maybe that, in the end, is what life—and death—are about.

Beyond the Arch

I watch you walk across the sloping lawn toward the vine-covered archway. You seemed a little nervous when we said goodbye, but now I see your steps grow more confident. Your bum knee isn't giving you as much trouble. Your back is straighter. Your arms swing wider.

It's selfish of me to want you here, I know. As if I didn't have enough of you, as if I won't remember you. There are others waiting who have missed you, too. They'll be happy to see you, and they'll be happy it took you so long to show up.

Are they already holding your hand? Do you hear glasses clinking and people laughing? Smell gravy cooking? Are you remembering things you'd forgotten you forgot? Are you learning things you always knew you never knew? Are you feeling things you've felt before, but nothing compared to what they feel like now? Is that why you're walking a little bit faster?

Just before the arch, you turn and wave to me. Your smile catches in the late afternoon sun. I blink and then you're through it, out of sight, leaving only slight indentations in the grass and a long shadow that hasn't reached me yet.

But one day it will, and then I'll know you again.

Amen.

Spine of Steel

> Those were the Rommely women: Mary, the mother, Evy,
> Sissy, and Katie, her daughters, and Francie, who would
> grow up to be a Rommely woman even though her name
> was Nolan. They were all slender, frail creatures with
> wondering eyes and soft fluttery voices. But they were made
> out of thin invisible steel.
>
> —Betty Smith, *A Tree Grows in Brooklyn*

The blue-eyed teen—Elena by birth, Helen in Americanese, Len
to her four brothers—wanted more than anything to sing. Blessed
with a clear, lovely voice, she sang around the house; she sang at
church; she sang in the hopes of being known for singing.

Her crowning achievement was having a solo lead in the
chorus at Helen Fleischer Vocational School, which she attended.
The group was practicing extra hard because they'd been
recruited to sing a jingle on the radio. A real jingle, for a real
company. And who would be featured but Len herself?

Every week her older brother Joe, a pleasant and dutiful
bodyguard, accompanied her on the trolley to practice, where
she let her voice soar out the open window on the assurance
that her big break was coming. Every week her immigrant parents
waved goodbye to her as she headed to Callowhill. Every
week the chorus got better, and the recording date drew nearer,
and Helen's dream grew bigger.

But when the day of the recording finally arrived, Helen's
mother stopped her on her way out the door. "You can't go,"
she said in Italian.

"Why?" Helen's hand tightened on the doorknob.

"Because you'll be discovered," her mother replied, "and
then you'll go into show business. No. You will not sing today."

Helen was the only daughter of immigrants, and only
daughters of immigrants do not say no. So she stayed home,
safe from the grasping clutch of immoral show business, wishing
she were caught.

Over the years I heard my grandmother tell the story of her big solo many times. The budding writer in me detected a twinge of resentment to her voice. She *could* have been a star, after all. In the space after the story closed, when Grandmom would bounce her hands in her lap and sigh in perpetual resignation, I always found myself willing her alternate universe to unfurl. I wanted Helen-the-teenager to sneak out of the house against her mother's wishes, to catch the trolley without the aid of her brother, to burst into the studio just as the suits were threatening to cancel the whole deal, and to trill in front of her astonished classmates, "I'm here, gentlemen! Shall we begin?" Cue music. Fame. Fulfillment.

Instead, she married at 18 and started having babies during wartime. She raised eight children, the oldest and youngest two decades apart. She worked nights at Strawbridge & Clothier to help make ends meet and exercised her considerable sewing skills on the side. Even after her retirement she cared for her dying mother and ailing brothers and boomerang children and my grandfather, always my grandfather, for nearly 70 years.

At her funeral service, the priest went into great detail about how Helen had done "exactly what God asked of her." She worked hard, gave abundantly, loved evidently, kept the faith, and sacrificed. Sacrificed, sacrificed, sacrificed.

Then my father, her son-in-law, gave a lovely tribute at the luncheon: "Ralph Waldo Emerson once said, 'An institution is the lengthened shadow of one man.' Helen's family is her institution. All of us here are her shadow." Shadow upon shadow upon shadow.

Behind my father a projector screen scrolled through photos of Helen spanning decades. Every time a new picture flicked up, I saw a different relative reflected in her face. In almost every picture she was laughing, smiling, playing at the beach, squeezing a baby. Baby after baby after baby.

When I look at my grandmother's long life, I cannot recognize one minute, much less a day, when someone didn't require her, a minute where she could escape for two seconds and be alone with her own thoughts and needs. A minute where she was wholly herself—not a wife, not a mother, just a Helen. What if she wanted more, or something else? Did it keep her up at night? Color her days? Recast her goals?

I am probably projecting my own concerns on a woman from a different generation who didn't have the time or energy to ask herself these questions. My concerns are the musings of someone overwhelmed by all the ways 90 years of life could go and terrified she will end up on a path she doesn't want, thwarted by bad timing, good intentions, or run-of-the-mill fate.

I sang at Helen's funeral Mass, as did several of my aunts and uncles. Despite my crying relatives and the priest's insistence on throat-closing incense, I kept it together throughout the service. Once the final organ chord faded, however, I stepped down from the altar and burst into the tears that had threatened since the moment I watched her casket closing and saw her favorite coffee mug tucked in the corner. One of my cousins appeared and let me sob on her shoulder.

"You did a great job up there," she said, handing me tissues. "It's so funny—everyone has the same voice. You can tell we're related."

Everyone has the same voice. That is, we have Helen's voice.

I will never know how my grandmother's life would have progressed had she performed her solo. I know what her life ultimately did entail: hard work, resilience, stubbornness, courage, sacrifice, faith, love. By all appearances she believed in herself and stood by her choices. Who am I, then, to question it?

I know this much: I bend at my waist, not with my knees. I use everything I have until five years past the end of its given life. I cook my meals from scratch. I sing with a natural vibrato. I firmly believe I know the best and most efficient way to do everything. I am Helen's granddaughter. And the same self-belief that fueled my grandmother—the same confidence in her abilities, even if the opportunity to exercise them wasn't always present or taken—is alive and well in me. We can make anything work, for we have spines of steel.

Now any time I'm at the beach or over my stove or on the porch—all sacred spaces to a woman who didn't have much space—I draw a deep breath and sing whatever solo strikes me. I take that moment on my grandmother's behalf, for any and all moments she had to miss, for any and all moments she managed to capture, and I thank her for showing me that I can become the woman—the person—I choose to be.

Say Hi to the Ocean for Me

You are already far out to sea, the farthest I've ever seen you. As I watch you swim, I think of the Hollywood starlet Esther Williams—elegant, timeless, at home in a fluid, unpredictable world.

I haven't earned my mermaid tail yet, so I remain land-locked, a subpar siren who shrieks at people she loves when she sees them dip beneath an unnerving wave the way you just did, dropping from my sight for a heart-halting minute.

The tides in their wisdom tell me I should let you go. But I'm afraid. Only a breath ago we were running our hands through the breakers, raising them high over our heads on our way back to the blanket, tucking into a cooler full of salami-and-Jersey-tomato sandwiches before our beach nap. Yet now the current flows between us with an undeniable strength only you are equipped to handle, as I am forced to watch and fret from shore.

Promise me that when you reach your destination—the one you're stroking toward, the one I can't yet see—you will turn around and wave twice. Promise me that after all your deep breathing and disciplined kicks, you will pull yourself up to rest and bask in the magnitude of what you've accomplished.

In the meantime, I will shade my eyes and follow you in memory alone, my gaze a lifeline you no longer need but will hold onto anyway, because that's what love is.

Amen.

The fear of death is why we build cathedrals, have children, declare war, and watch cat videos online at three A.M.
　　　—Caitlin Doughty, *Smoke Gets in Your Eyes: And Other Lessons from the Crematory*

Fragmented

broken
detached
not whole

isolated
unfinished
what remains

dust
molecules
ashes to ashes

poetry
music
love, shattering

pieces at peace in you

Amen.

The Fear of Dead Things

Tonight marks the first frost of the season. The second crop of carrots in our garden are shivering underground; the dogged Swiss chard bares its stalks to the sharp chill. I am wearing a turtleneck and sitting under a blanket and drinking tea, trying to avoid the truth that all around me things are dying.

Over the summer I had the opportunity to speak to my first acquisitions editor at a mid-size publisher. I was certain I had unwrapped my golden ticket for a book deal. I created a non-fiction proposal and had a promising conversation. I strived to assume nothing, but hope greased the track of imagination, and soon I was envisioning the moment when my box of first-edition hardcovers would arrive on the front porch.

Then came the brief email explaining that though my writing was beautiful, the sales team didn't think there was enough of a market. Ah, yes. Publishing is a business, not a Medici-level system of patronage. My disappointment consumed me, and my hope shriveled within it, dead on a once-vital vine.

We are in an endless state of dying. People are dying—some naturally, most needlessly—as the pandemic rages. Our earth is dying, seasonally in some places, unnaturally worldwide as climate change accelerates. And while each national election brings half the country relief, not so the other half, and we face our dying idealism about how quickly we might move forward and how differently we all define "forward."

Christian writer and thinker Charaia Callabrass says, "God is not afraid of dead things."[1] Which means God is not afraid of my strangled hope. My impotent rage. My wide-ranging griefs. My sincere disappointments. My egoistic losses. My dashed plans. God is not afraid of anything that has burned to the ground, whether in a scorching blaze or whimpering embers. For what is death to a God who, as Callabrass frames it, chooses to sit with us in our ashes?

And if God is not afraid of dead things, why am I? Do I fear the dead thing itself? Do I fear what leads to the ashes? Or do I fear what might rise from them?

I ponder this now as my tea cools, my blanket warms, and somewhere in the dark backyard the chard prevails. Tomorrow marks another start, another first day after death. In the morning I will see what lives, and I will join it.

Around the Campfire

Grief felt. Unloaded. Flooded. Released. Avoided. Acknowledged.

Joy discovered. Welcomed. Created. Manufactured. Shared. Deferred.

Anger simmered. Ignored. Stoked. Sublimated. Boiled. Doused.

Hope nurtured. Summoned. Forgotten. Feared. Invited. Desired.

For every emotion traipsing through me, help me treat it as I would a campfire in the clearing—with heat to feel, flames to corral, and power to yield with wisdom.

Amen.

Speak Life

Speak life.

You can sing it or shout it or whisper it—whatever your cords are built for.

But speak it nonetheless. Give it full voice. Such is your duty, your mandate, your privilege.

For to remain silent is to disappear, trace no mark, leave no ripple. But to speak . . . that is to write your name in the stars.

Amen.

Lament:
Why Does My Soul Hurt?

Wave the White Flag

I am defeated, God. I am broken, and sad, and lonely. Lift me up, if only for a moment.

Amen.

Suspense is worse than disappointment.

—Robert Burns

Well Disappointed

Nurse my heart and nurture my wisdom in this sad moment, God. Arm me not with the superficial affirmation I crave, but with the profound conviction of my worth and dignity that I lack.

I'm sure there are times you are disappointed with me for my ridiculous decisions or wayward routes. To sin, after all, is to miss the mark. Yet you always respond with your indefatigable hope that next time will be better—that next time I will strike the mark in my sights.

With a healthy dose of that hope before us, please stay with me through my red eyes, used tissues, and tossing-turning nights. May I, in return, focus my energy and attention on you, so that I transform this disappointment into redemption.

Thanks for the otherworldly shoulder to cry on.

Amen.

News Fatigue

The news has worn me out. What noisy, noisome times we're facing. Everyone's sniping; no one's moderating.

The worst part? The grim tumult has reached such a fever pitch that I can't hear you. You could be whooping within the thick of the fray, whistling over the frenzy, whispering to me as I struggle to quiet my mind for sleep. Hell if I can tell.

But even if my ears can't pick you out, my heart can. And it somehow knows you're helping the canary warble from the coal mine's depths. Please keep the little guy singing, God. Its hope is music to us all.

Amen.

Ends of Days

Apocalypse now? Later? Sometime next Tuesday? I don't care. Bring it. I've got a million things to accomplish, and frankly, it would be easier if you pulled the plug on the whole shebang as soon as possible.

Hence my prayer for the ends of days. For that precarious point after dinner and before dreamtime when the mortal coil slips around my neck. For my hubris in thinking those few hours can somehow add up to more than 24. For the steady calendar movement that insists on marching even when I'm stumbling.

If you are seriously thinking about ending it soon, then please prepare me for acceptance. Prepare me for accountability. Prepare me for awe. But if we've got some time left, maybe just prepare me for bed?

Amen.

Unfair Play

God, I don't believe you have a heavenly spin-the-wheel printed with our 7 billion names that you turn once a day to find out who gets to suffer.

But with the way life plays out in tragedy, coincidence, and straight-up rotten luck, I have to ask: Is there any way you can intervene without stepping on our free will? Please don't leave us begging for miracles at a chilly, empty altar. Match our impotence with your omnipotence. Share whatever tools you can, be it a counselor's wise comfort, a surgeon's deft hands, or a friend's willing ear.

I accept that life is not fair. But I will not accept that you are not here.

Amen.

Hard Knocks

For the people who live one step forward, two steps back

Who struggle to make ends meet

Who never seem to catch a break

Who create, inherit, or live amid misfortune

Who wake up every morning in fear of what the day will bring

Who search for a leg up, but wind up kicked

Who try their damnedest, yet feel damned

Who leak vital spirit and optimism with every blow

Who are angry at you for judgments and hardship they believe you send:

I pray they recognize your empathy and draw solace from your heartbreak over them.

Amen.

Show me a hero and I will write you a tragedy.
                                        —F. Scott Fitzgerald

The Face of Tragedy

Annoyance is relative. Suffering is relative. Tragedy is not.

Tragedy is absolute. It upends the natural order. It halts daily life. It carries great loss. It bears misfortune. In its powerful eddy, we find ourselves swirling first in disbelief, then in shock, then in terror.

Abandonment. Betrayal. Catastrophe. Disaster. All terrible states that carry despair with them like a shroud. No wonder many suffocate beneath the weight. And why, God, are some lives more tragic than others? I've done nothing to deserve less. Others have done nothing to deserve more.

But then I see the family albums. The community events. The donations. The memorial services. The phone messages. They all poke holes in that doomed cloud so that for a brief moment, fresh air enters the living tomb.

God whom we devastate with our tears, expand our lungs to gulp hope. Help us picture the world of comfort signaled by those pricks of light. Though tragic flaws exist around us and within us, they do not have to govern us. We can and will move forward, as long as your compassion goes ahead.

Amen.

Headbreaker

I journaled
I dialogued
I visioned
I daydreamed
I stewed
I simmered
I bit my nails
I chewed my lip
I overshared
I buttoned up
I ate a carton of ice cream

But then my head exploded.

And because I exhausted
all other possibilities
and myself
now I have to pray:

I am here.
I am lost.
I am yours.
Can you help?

Amen.

Midwinter Blues

I pray today for get-up-and-go.

I pray today I sally forth.

I pray today is once more unto the breach.

Because my chilled bones are weary. I yearn for Vitamin D. My very skin hurts to flex. I strain to fulfill everything you call me to do, yet I end up frozen and discouraged, with nothing to show but shopping bags beneath my eyes.

Soon the man-made hours will reverse course, and your God-made rhythms will return light to my life. But until the rays hit my eyes, dispel the shadows in my heart and restore my soul to sunlit glory.

Amen.

The Beast

The beast sat on my chest again last night. It leaned its hairy haunches on my lungs and ground its knuckles into my eyes—to keep its balance, it claimed, but I know it did it for spite.

The beast muttered and snickered the whole night. Its raspy whispers filled the inky quiet. When I tossed, the beast turned. When I sighed, it blew a raspberry.

Every time a pleasant dream crept closer, the beast batted it away. Soon, a pile collected near the bed, still fluttering, quickly fading.

I am not fond of the beast.

Please hold the beast in the hallway, God, just for tonight. Leave my pillow free for my cheek alone. Keep my sheets untangled. Help my peaceful dreams approach in their gentle, tender way. Let me float in them toward a resolution I can't imagine yet must somehow realize.

Amen.

What Now

I'm comparing *what is* to *what was*, *what was* to *what will be*, *what will be* to *what might be*—and coming up with a great big pile of worry and fret and all-around suck.

But *what is* can exceed *what was*. *What was* is not a given harbinger of *what will be*. And the presumptuous certainty of *what will be* bows to the flexible potential of *what might be*.

Please don't let me become the hand-wringer in the corner who always grouses, "Now what?" Make me instead the clear-eyed explorer who always asks, "What now?" and strides forward whether I have an answer or not.

For *what is* holds the true adventure, and the *why* is you.

Amen.

Growth:

Why Is Change the Only Constant?

Unexpect the Expected

If change is the only constant, you'd think I'd be used to it by now.

Yet nature seems to abhor comfort. Security, consistency, predictability—all have bearing in our lives, but are no means as dependable as we wish them to be.

It's not such a bad thing. Having a wolf at your door can help you move faster, think smarter, act stronger.

Wouldn't it be lovely, though, if you could be fast/smart/strong without the wolf? Just act that way all the time, on your own, in good times and bad? How much would we accomplish then, I wonder. How much could we achieve and dream and grasp?

God, help me unexpect the expected. Grant me the wisdom to understand—and I mean really understand—that life is change, and I change with it, not merely in response to it. Keep the wolf at my mind rather than at my door—a prowling, pacing reminder that we don't need to live in fear, we just need to live aware. And I pray that when the expected expires, and the known is no more, that you stay by my side and refocus me on the most dependable comforts out there: your love and your grace.

Amen.

Anticipation

For changes others force upon me
And for ones I design with accountability

For changes wrought by others' indecision or confusion
And for ones wrought by my own

For changes incurred by my lethargy
And for ones my responses spur

For changes I slough off onto others' shoulders
And for ones I accept with reluctance, courage, or both

For all the changes that insist on changing just as I start to
grasp them,
I ask for grace on the roller coaster ride and pray I find you in
the front car.

In the name of the One who laughs when I plan—

Amen.

The Best Waylaid Plans

The saved chocolate that melts in your pocket
The wrong turn from the outdated map
The late train shuttle on a chilly morning
The conversation that sounded better when you rehearsed it in
your head
The leftovers gone bad in an empty fridge
The battery dead, the charging cord forgotten,
The black ice patch on a thawing sidewalk
The tiny umbrella that can't protect your backpack from
winter rain

    Become instead

An experimental dessert
An impromptu adventure
A chance to stretch your legs
A surprising revelation
An excuse to order pizza
A prompt to write a letter
A little rest on the ground
An incentive to get home

    Which says to me

That maybe
My reframing
Was always
And exactly
Your hope.

Amen.

A Note on the (Once Again Predicted) End of the World

Tomorrow, it is said, the world will end
and with it go long DMV lines,
taking off your shoes at airports, trying to
negotiate with cable companies.

Tomorrow, we've been told, the world will end
and take along its heartbreaks, large and small—
its dying kids, its bloody wars, the fears
that seep and creep beneath our dull routines.

Tomorrow. That's the date the world will end.
Yet so will evening walks and long road trips,
first kisses, last goodbyes, the million songs
we've yet to hear or write or partner up to.

Tomorrow, they despair, the world will end.
But not the joy we serve at laden tables.
Not the hope we pass from hand to hand.
And never love. Mere worlds cannot end that.

Appointment

God beyond all day planners:

Please work in terms I understand, and circle for me a date when I can start fresh. Except maybe not completely fresh, because I didn't know anything when I started the first time around and I had to learn as I went and I'm pretty sure that's where I ran into trouble.

Except maybe not completely in the know, either, because I have enjoyed discovering life as I go and I run into adventure as much as danger and I like to think there's more of that in store.

Anyway, circle a date. Not for a reckoning or rapture; more for an evaluation. A touch base. A "hey, how you doing, what's next" sort of vibe.

If it's on my calendar, I'll be there. I hope you will be there, too.

Until then—

Amen.

Say Something

That feeling is back. The itchy, can't-get-comfortable one.

It's the feeling I get when I'm caught in the middle yet out of the loop. When I'm thankful for what I have but annoyed it's not what I wanted. When I have no idea how anything's going to turn out yet I struggle to control it anyway.

Such a bewildering, squirmy, gray state to be in. My mind knows what is good, but my heart can't muster the strength to agree. Or my heart is certain, but my mind waffles.

I sympathize with the betrayer and the betrayed. I yell and plead in the same breath. I feel guilty for nothing and everything.

Distinctive God, I sift through daily conflicts and questions to find the definitive answer. But what I really need is a defining for myself: a glimpse, a word, anything that captures this feeling in an active moment and shows me its form. Like photographing a shadow as it plays along the wall.

When the flash does go off, help me see this limbo emotion has limits, and grant me the strength to press beyond them for true illumination.

Amen.

Milestone

Industrious God,

It takes a lot of work for us to reach a milestone—
A lot of late nights,
A lot of dedication,
A lot of sacrifice.

And it takes a lot of help from you to get us there—
A lot of forgiveness,
A lot of patience,
A lot of love.

But my real transformation happens between the mile markers at all-too-brief pit stops when I finally have the space to see how far I've come, how far remains, and how far gone I'd be without you navigating.

At these moments, grant me stillness, God. When I resume the trip, may it be with faith rested and sight restored so I can find my way to where you wait.

Amen.

Hold Me

For one moment
Hold me upended
Apart from routine
So I can watch it pass
And remember that it
Is not what's sacred

For one moment
Hold me suspended
Apart from the world
So I can watch it spin
And remember that I
Contribute to its cycle

For one moment
Hold me ascended
Apart from despair
So I can watch my soul
And remember that you
Created it for joy

Amen.

SIX

Compassion: How Can I Make My Heart Bigger?

The Urgency of Compassion

Since casting my first vote years ago, I have watched every election—national, state, local—spiral further into a partisan fear of "the other." We have channeled our apprehension and misunderstanding into denigrating, labeling, stereotyping, judging, and avoiding. These behaviors are not limited by geography or ideology. Except for the very saintly among us—and believe me, sisters and brothers, I am not in that number—no one is exempt.

Psychologist and artist Anne Truitt reflected on this phenomenon in her book *Daybook: The Journal of an Artist*:

> I notice that I have to pay careful attention in order to listen to others with an openness that allows them to be as they are, or as they think themselves to be. The shutters of my mind habitually flip open and click shut, and these little snaps form into patterns I arrange for myself. The opposite of this inattention is love, is the honoring of others in a way that grants them the grace of their own autonomy and allows mutual discovery.

I'm with Truitt in theory, less so in practice. When I attempt sincere attention, I find it challenging to see the person before me first as a human being, with all the dignity, complexity, and frailty that entails. Equally challenging is recognizing that same dignity, complexity, and frailty in myself. Then I must accept that we each hold values, beliefs, convictions, and perspectives that may or may not overlap and regardless will be prioritized and weighted differently. And then the real kicker: I must approach this hard, uncomfortable process with love.

The whole endeavor is like preparing for travel to a foreign country. You read up on the basics—common phrases, transportation options, recommended lodging—before you dive into the place's more intricate nuances, the ones not immediately apparent to the outsider. These layers of discovery can bring pleasure. You're exposed to new sights, sounds, people, and ideas, and you learn more about yourself too: your own strengths, weaknesses, and abilities. But such discovery can also be terrifying. You are pushed outside your comfort zone, confronted with the limits of your understanding, and asked to justify what you believe to be true.

When outside my comfort zone, I'm learning that compassion is a reliable guidebook. As Henri Nouwen, Donald McNeill, and Douglas Morrison defined it in *Compassion: A Reflection on the Christian Life*, "[compassion] is not a bending toward the under-privileged from a privileged position; it is not a reaching out from on high to those who are less fortunate below; it is not a gesture of sympathy or pity for those who fail to make it on the upward pull. On the contrary, compassion means going directly to those people and places where suffering is most acute and building a home there."

Applying this framing to our nation's toxic discourse, the questions for me become: Am I willing to build a home in an ideological war zone? Am I able to remember that vulnerable people span races, creeds, sexuality/gender, socioeconomic status, party lines, and voting choices? Am I honest enough to admit that I too am vulnerable in my own ways? Do I have enough courage to accept these truths, enough compassion to invite the conversation, and enough love to listen?

My mandate, to borrow Truitt's words, is to honor others— to extend the same grace I receive. Listening is a start. Then I will practice hearing. Pondering. Acting. Otherwise I risk barreling into a pitch-black room with a blindfold on, swinging wildly, and with so many real dangers present in the world, now is not the time for shadow boxing. Now is the time to train my heart to punch above its weight.

Instructions for Escaping the Cave

1. Grope the ground in the dark.
2. Find the stick of dynamite.
3. Find the match.
4. Strike the match.
5. Find the spot on the cave wall that seems a shade less black than the false night surrounding you.
6. Place the dynamite near the hopeful spot.
7. Light the fuse.
8. Don't retreat.
9. Don't close your eyes.
10. Don't cover your ears.
11. Watch the stick explode.
12. Feel the ground shudder.
13. Absorb the shock of falling rocks.
14. Note the jagged hole created.
15. Crawl through.
16. Bring your scrapes and bruises with you.
17. Listen to the birds you could not hear before.
18. Remember that they, and you, are alive.
19. Rejoice.

Amen.

Heartwarming

It's a truth universally acknowledged that a person in want of a bus will wait longer on frigid nights. That was the case last week when I turned to ice waiting for the N4 after my voice lesson. Though it was only 7:15 pm, the winter evening had already soaked in cold ink for a couple of hours. I tucked myself into a corner of the stop to block the wind, which helped for about four minutes. The more often I craned my neck to see if the bus was coming, the faster I lost sensation in my fingers and toes. When the bus finally arrived, I leaped on and sat as far from the doors as possible.

When I transferred to the metro, I passed two men huddled in the entryway. One man crouched next to a busted suitcase packed with what I presumed were his only possessions. The other man was laying on the concrete wrapped in city-issued blankets. Both wore old parkas, black hats, and thin gloves.

At first sight, I thought, "I should buy them a hot sandwich." But I didn't. When I crossed the entryway, I thought, "Or a coffee." But I didn't. When I stepped onto the escalator, I thought, "You really should stop. At least offer it to them." But I didn't. At the edge of the station platform, I thought, "Now or never. Think how bad the bus stop felt for 30 minutes. Now imagine 8 hours of that. Help them." Even then, I didn't.

Instead, I swiped my metro card to ride a heated train home, where it took a hot meal, two sweaters, and three more degrees on the thermostat to defrost me before bed. And when I arrived back at the train station the next morning for work, I did not think to look at the corner and see if the men were still there.

What stopped me from stopping that night? Why did I let the cold reach my heart?

Heat, Hear, Heart

God of white-hot light—

Heat my constricted heart so that it expands beyond its natural boundaries and blooms in the presence of those who most need its compassion.

Illuminate the creeping corners I refuse to examine so that I finally confront my inadequacies and leave them to evaporate in the noonday sun.

Ignite in me a passion for justice so that "your will be done" ceases to be a rote recitation and instead becomes my clarion call for action in an unbalanced world.

You manifest as a pillar of fire to demand our attention. Demand it of me now. I wish to extinguish it no more.

Amen.

Count to Three

When I know I should act, give me courage to do so.

When I act as I should, give me grace to do more.

Turn my fear into fuel, and make my second guess the final one.

Amen.

On the Mother Emanuel Shootings of 2015

Seven years have passed since Dylann Storm Roof killed nine people at a Bible study at Emanuel African Methodist Episcopal Church in Charleston, South Carolina, and to this day, I cannot stop placing myself in the middle of that group.

Bible studies traditionally provide time and space for contemplation, offering guided meditation, academic exercise, and community bonding all in one. To think that a man, a stranger, sat in the participants' midst for an entire sixty minutes before opening fire boggles my mind. Did the spirit of devotion and love move him at all? Did Mother Emanuel's community sway him, even for a second, to reconsider his actions? Did an opportunity for grace present itself to him? Or was he so sodden with hate, rage, and pain that not the smallest chink of light got through?

I will never know because I am not Dylann Storm Roof. I was not sitting in the church that day listening to the words they were poring over. I do not know how loudly God was weeping, trying to push aside Roof's pitch-dark fury, desperate to reach his heart.

What I can do instead is turn the questions inward. Whenever tragedies strike—when I can no longer turn a blind eye to the worst elements of humanity—I force myself to ask, "What hate am I carrying? What prejudice? What fear?" In essence, how am I failing to love? Because the one rule above all is "love your neighbor as yourself."

Love your neighbor, even when he is wrong.

Love your neighbor, even when she scares you.

Love your neighbor, even when you hate them.

No Words

I have no words left
none to ease the pain
none to soothe the grief
none to stop the violence
except for the hardest ones of all:
I love you
I love You
I love.

Amen.

When a Gryffindor Becomes a Hufflepuff

"Hufflepuff? Hell no."

I had taken two Hogwarts House quizzes in quick succession to find that both returned the badger. Buzzfeed quizzes are easy to dismiss, but scientific personality quizzes? Much less so, even when tied to a fictional wizarding school.

Since the minute I began reading the Harry Potter series in my teens, I identified with Gryffindor House. Students there were brave. They took action. They won the Hogwarts house cup practically every year. They were the leaders and strivers I'd always pictured myself to be, the noble ruling class of a high school environment where bullying paled in comparison to the threats of the Dark Lord. Hufflepuffs, on the other hand, struck me as bland background helpers, acquiescent hangers-on who trailed the more charismatic Gryffindors and helped fill plot holes where necessary. I never considered them the heroes, not even of their own stories.

You can imagine then how the quiz results sent me into a minor tailspin. First I was dismayed. Then I was dismayed I was dismayed. After all, what's not to like about the house values of "hard work, patience, loyalty, and fair play?" I believe in these qualities; I seek out people who espouse them; I like to think I espouse a few myself. Why would identifying with these traits be a bad thing?

Because I want to be something else. That's why.

The truth is, I have always wanted to be the hero. I want to display courage and grit. I want to be the first responder in a battle, the one who inspires confidence and unity by stepping forward when everyone else is quaking. I want to be carried forth on shoulders and have songs written and sung about me.

But what I want and who I am are two different things. I am not as courageous as I imagine myself to be. I often hang back and let others go first. I take cautious risks. Glory does not come easily or instantly, if at all. And when I do summon the nerve to step forward, I often trample on others' toes.

I needed the validation of a third quiz, so I took the "official" Pottermore Sorting Hat quiz, a vague interactive widget that's tough to game, and it returned—Gryffindor. "Vindication!" was my first thought. Close on its heels, though, was "Huh." A mere 30 minutes into considering myself a Hufflepuff, I was already mourning its loss. Was it really so awful to learn I have goodness in me and, in almost the same moment, that I could stand to practice more of that set's humility? The world desperately needs kindness. So much so that showing warmth is becoming its own courageous, defiant act. Maybe that's the nexus where I am being sorted—to become a Gryffinpuff or Huffledor, someone who does not let one trait define her but rather embraces all she might offer.

As I review the Hogwarts houses with the eyes of a 30-something, I now recognize the nuance I blew past in my exuberant, know-it-all adolescence: each house's positive qualities have shadow sides, too. Yes, Gryffindors are bold, but they don't always think before acting. Hufflepuffs are meek but sometimes to the point of passivity. In this respect the houses (and the magical Sorting Hat that puts people in them) become a cautionary tale: know your strengths, acknowledge your weaknesses, and never assume you have only one path.

The beauty of the Sorting Hat is that it takes both capabilities and intent into account. We are who we are, and we also have power to become who we want to be. What can be more full of promise, more packed with magic, than that?

Of What Sort Are You?

I am the sort of muggle who ignores you, God of sorting. I strain and pull to keep your brim from circling my brow, and even when you're firmly placed, I wiggle out of what you're guiding me to do and be.

But now my name has (yet again) been called, and I come up (yet again) before my peers—friends and enemies alike—to answer your consistent call. Stick me to the stool this time, God of purest magic. Bid me listen; bid me learn.

Amen.

To Be Used

You made us to be used.

Though we have beautiful elements, we are not decorative.
Though we have distinct forms, we are designed for function.
Though we have keen minds, we are soul first.

In a world shrinking with each transaction,
amid oceans evaporating into steam,
with people starving, striving, succeeding at each bend,
we forget we come from dust
and to dust we will return.

Remind us of our muddy birth.
Tug our roots toward the stranger
in defiance of humanity's crude borders.
Smear clay on our eyes, palms, and soles
so we can see through walls, push aside mountains,
and prove useful in your eyes.

Amen.

Rooted

I have no leaves, no branches, no bark or stem or petal. But I have roots that originate in some primordial cave where individualism was not yet invented and connectedness was the natural order.

My roots start at the spot in my chest that leaps when I near home. They snake through my legs and grip the soil in places that make my heart sing. They radiate—stealthy, subtle sentinels—in constant search for others' cords to earth.

Source of all beings solid and growing, you have designed us to be entwined. Help my roots go deeper. Tangle them in knots and twists so I am that much stronger. Show me what it means to truly stand with others.

Amen.

SEVEN
Justice: How Can I Help?

What Jury Duty Taught Me About
the Nature of Justice

"Madame Foreperson, have you reached a verdict?"

The court clerk was staring at me. I stood up, sealed envelope in hand, and answered on behalf of 11 other people, "I have." I handed the envelope to her. She handed it to the judge. The judge wrestled with the seal for a minute, pulled out five papers that had my signature on them, and began to read.

"One count of robbery: guilty. One count of robbery: guilty. One count of abduction: guilty. One count of abduction with intent to defile: guilty. One count of statutory burglary: guilty."

Each "guilty" dropped like an anvil in the center of the courtroom. I didn't look at the counsel, the victims, or the defendant. I just kept my eyes trained on our calm judge, for whom putting people away was routine. In contrast to her, I was ready to hurl all over the scales of justice.

The jury summons had come a month earlier. It was the first summons I had ever been able to fulfill, so on the appointed day I bounced into the Arlington Circuit Court overflowing with civic pride and expectations of *Law & Order*-like proceedings.

When my name was called to join the juror pool, I did my utmost to demonstrate integrity and impartiality, as I had a feeling somewhere deep in my fate barometer that I was destined to serve on this jury. My vigorous nodding and laser eye focus did the trick; within a couple hours the trial had begun, and I was in the jury box along for the ride.

It was a criminal case. An American man stood accused of breaking into a Best Western and robbing two older, Canadian tourists (a mother and a daughter) on one of their regular road trips through the lower 48. The Commonwealth of Virginia was prosecuting on the victims' behalf.

Evidence was circumstantial at best, resting largely on the eyewitness testimony of two women who said the accused man had covered them with hotel blankets most of the time the robbery took place. Security camera footage was fuzzy. Paperwork was patchy or inconsistent. Though the prosecutor was polished and dramatic, his theatrics couldn't gloss over the thinning facts. And the defense, though they had several opportunities to highlight the lack of facts, seemed to favor red herrings instead.

By the end of two days, having absorbed approximately 10 testimonies and lots of counsel posturing, I didn't feel much clearer than when we'd started. The definition of "beyond a reasonable doubt" kept replaying in my mind: "The standard that must be met by the prosecution's evidence in a criminal prosecution: that no other logical explanation can be derived from the facts except that the defendant committed the crime, thereby overcoming the presumption that a person is innocent until proven guilty."[2]

The prosecution hadn't convinced me this man had done it. I could still think of a few other logical explanations. And I wasn't about to convict someone on "likely" or "probable." *How can the other jurors feel any differently?* I thought. Surely deliberations would take 30 minutes. With that, the judge dismissed us, and we headed back to the chilly jury room.

We were a group of twelve, with nine men and three women. Most were at least 40. A couple of us were around 30. Everyone struck me as educated and pleasant. The clerk instructed us to choose a foreman. The other jurors clasped their hands and looked around expectantly. No one stepped forward. Hating silence, I raised my hand. "I haven't done this before," I said in an attempt to set reasonable expectations, lest I derail the entire legal process while on a learning curve. "But I'll do my best." Everyone nodded and smiled. It was time to begin.

Contrary to my confident assumption, the jury was split: six convinced that the circumstantial evidence was sufficient and the eyewitness testimony reliable, and six convinced that the case hadn't been proved beyond a reasonable doubt. Open and shut it was not.

I started covering the white board with notes and lists. People wandered around the nippy room clutching coffee cups. We watched the surveillance footage on a locked-down laptop. We discussed different styles of skull caps and debated about what warranted "suspicious behavior." I noticed a few people had tendencies to veer into procedural-drama-type speculations, as if we were playing at *CSI*. Everyone stayed fairly calm, except for a tense moment when one juror erased half of a discussion list and another juror chewed him out. I rewrote the list. The first juror apologized. The second one stewed. On we went. After two hours and a lunch break we were split 9-3. After two more hours, 12-0, unanimous in our stated belief that he had indeed been proven guilty.

What gnawed at me, however, was this question: How can we truly know? How can we as humans sit in judgment of others when we weren't present, when we bring our own prejudices and experiences to the table, and when we are expected to reach decisions with a set number of other strangers? I know I had been totally consumed by the victims' emotions, the prosecutor's intensity, the defendant's silence, the judge's soothing oversight; surely these elements swayed other jurors, too? Or maybe our ultimate unanimity wasn't even rooted in anything profound. Maybe people felt tired, or hungry, or eager to pick up their kids from daycare, so they said yes simply to get a move on. A mind-boggling number of factors played into this significant decision, and this group, gathered for a singular moment in time, would never be able to tease apart our reasons—or reverse the decision's course.

Yet here we were, ready to rule.

The clerk brought in the verdict forms and handed them to me. Each required me to handwrite in our decision and then sign it on behalf of the group. I spread out the five forms in front of me—simple Word docs that had been printed off in a back office and were now about to alter the course of a man's life.

We voted around the table once more on each count, just to make sure we were all in agreement. The chatty group lapsed into a sober silence. The only sound was my pen scratching. I thought about the weird fact that these forms would probably go into a vault somewhere until fire or the march of time destroyed them, and that my signature was forever linked to them.

The pit in my stomach deepened. A terrible rush of adrenaline surged through my body. My vision swam for a split second, and my hands turned to ice. I knew in that moment that I held a power I'd never wanted. Still, I finished signing them, and we went into the courtroom to share our decision.

As the prosecution revealed immediately following our verdict, the defendant did have prior crimes on his record—gun possession, sexual assault, robbery, to name a few. He'd already been in jail before, too. I could feel some of the burden lift from the jurors' shoulders (or maybe it was just mine?), as the fact he had a record seemed to increase the probability of his guilt.

Ultimately, the judge sentenced the defendant to 95 years. We jurors packed our bags, put on our coats, and headed our separate ways. Only then did I realize I'd never learned everyone's names. We'd been unintentional yet complicit partners in anonymity, sharing these three days, this major decision, and nothing more. I felt a little lonely as I headed toward the metro. Who else would understand?

I know now why we have so many law dramas depicted on film. Where besides the courtroom is human nature on such bald display? What else so well encapsulates our hubris, missteps, hope, desperation, fear, elation, and indecision? We can discuss why we as a society choose to levy justice or why justice might be best left to a higher, more final authority. All I know is how my stomach felt when I signed and handed over the verdict forms. I think I made the right decision. I hope I did.

Judgment Day

Whenever I'm asked to sit in judgment, God, let it be with full faculties, deep humility, wide discernment, and a firm grasp of my own imperfection so that I understand the impossibility of sitting in judgment at all.

Amen.

Ignoring the Summons

Sister Dianna Ortiz, the American Ursuline nun who survived brutal torture at the hands of U.S.-backed Guatemalan death squads in 1989, once lamented a "parade of apathy, deaf to God's insistent call." In her view, apathy was "the shroud of unprincipled darkness which is a failure to live out the Gospel."[3] No word-mincing there. To nurture apathy to others' suffering is not merely to rebuff God's call; it is to deny it.

Working from my Christian tradition, I understand that my Gospel responsibility is to relinquish my security and build a home in suffering. But as a friend said in my small faith group (to clarify: the group is small, though perhaps so is my faith), "I know what I need to do. It's the doing that's hard."

Why do I often refuse to take the next step? I, wrangler of to-do lists, manager of projects, queen of incremental progress, am no stranger to plotting a path forward. When it comes to heeding God's call, though, I am somehow always stymied—feet leaden, mind frozen, heart hardened.

To spur me to action, I consider the blunt words of Josephite priest and radical activist Fr. Philip Berrigan: "Hope is where your ass is." Philip and his brother Daniel, a Jesuit, were the first Catholic priests to oppose the Vietnam War with civil disobedience, including burning draft files and defacing two nuclear warheads on the production line of a General Electric plant. Philip spent a number of years in jail for his nonviolent activism but always emerged ready to put his body back on the line. He embodied what his acolyte, theologian Ched Myers, calls "incarnational discipleship."[4]

If I were asked, "Where is your ass these days?" my honest answer would be, "On the couch." When the day comes that I can answer that question with literal skin in the game, I will know I have taken a stronger step toward God's call. Right now I am a housebound old lady nervous of any knock at her door. But the louder the knocking grows, and the longer it continues without rest, the more I must acknowledge it. As of today, I have made it to the peephole. My hand is poised over the deadbolt. Will I trust God enough to unlock it?

To Live as an Open Wound

To live the Gospel is to live as an open wound—raw, gushing, muscle torn and bone exposed. No tourniquet can staunch it. No bandage can bind it. For faith is weapon and treatment both, a battle cry and lullaby, a charge and a destiny. The wound is Love; its cure, the same.

Amen.

When Do I Get to Quit the World?

I'm tired. Soul-achingly tired. Worn to a nub by the madness of this world and particularly of my country. Exhausted by hate, ignorance, destruction of lives. Overwhelmed by our society's deep, persistent darkness.

"God, when do I get to quit the world?" I keep asking with each day's news cycle, each fresh slap across the many faces of the Divine.

I keep asking because deep down I'm hoping for a different answer than the one I already know, which is, I do not get to quit the world. I do not get to curl up in a fetal position with a bag of Goldfish and my Netflix account on auto-play. The still, small voice has demanded I engage. It has practically handed me a to-do list:

1. Educate myself.
2. Learn with others.
3. Confront tragedy.
4. Name injustice.
5. Examine the dark corners.
6. Stretch my belief.
7. Gulp my faith.
8. Speak truth out loud.
9. Live "I love you."
10. Begin. Today.

Determine the Sequel

The cover of *The World* has fallen off, and its pages have come unglued. I have read and reread the text expecting a different ending, yet the plot always moves me toward the same conclusion: there is no other way the narrative can unfold. Not when the characters are so relatable and their decisions so poor.

The World Vol. 2, however, does not yet exist. What if I get to work writing it? Maybe the sequel will have the ending I want. The ending you intended. The ending that all who love will create.

Amen.

If Not Now, When? And If Not Me, Then Who?

> Who knows—perhaps it was for a time like this that you
> became queen?
> —Esther 4:14

I knew we'd struck a nerve when the meeting we had hoped
would attract 15 people drew 50.

The initial circle of chairs my friends and I had set up in the
middle of the echoing church hall kept growing until it took up
two-thirds of the room. The women who arrived earliest patiently
obliged our constant reshuffling, moving their purses and bags
five times before we settled. The women who arrived last found
exactly the number of empty seats required, as if Elijah himself
had instructed us on the mechanics of predictive chair allotment.
And every time we added a chair or a person, we caught one
another's eyes with an incredulous look that communicated,
"OH MY GOD," followed by collective kvelling.

I often encounter the nonprofit jargon "growing the circle"
in my day job, but until this meeting I had not witnessed a circle's literal growth—the experience of seeing new faces appear
at your side, feeling your wildest hopes pushed at the seams,
experiencing your heart expanding in direct proportion to the
number of squeaking, rickety chairs. Such was the gift of this
meeting: the discovery of a modern-day red tent in which everyone was welcome and all could fit.

But I should back up.

Our gathering, the first meeting of the Sisterhood of Progressive Christians (a group conceived by my friends), was a direct
response to our challenging times. It was a call to women to
organize—as they always do, as they always must—and become
the change they wish to see. It was an opportunity to wrestle
with the unanswerable questions, to dialogue with God about
our individual and collective purpose, and to do it all within a
loving, seeking, vulnerable-in-the-best-way community.

As we went around the fifty-woman-wide circle that night, our calls, responses, and questions steadily thickened the space between us:

I'm a mother/grandmother/mother-to-be.
I'm a church philanderer.
I'm a patriot.
I want to reconcile my faith with my politics.
I want to find a middle way.
I want to engage with loved ones with differing views.
I want to affect the federal and state legislature.
I've never felt this embarrassed to be a Christian.
I want to reclaim the label.
I can't be silent anymore.
There is danger in silence.
We've lost the art of conversation.
We're looking for a voice.
God will use me as a bridge.
You can follow Jesus and work for social justice.
What kind of Mecca do I want to make for me?
The only thing that makes me feel better is acting.
Inaction is not an option.
Faith and facts are not mutually exclusive.
The tide is not necessarily against us.
We must end intolerance and bigotry.
We're all called to authenticity.
We must make it a movement, not just a moment.

Over it all hung one daunting question: Are we willing to be Christ's hands and feet and build God's Kingdom here on earth? I left that night on fire with my answer of YES! The next day it was *Yes!* The day after that—*yes*. A week later . . . *I think?*

In order to keep saying YES at full volume—to become the hands that feed the hungry and the feet that walk with the outcast and the body that puts itself on the line for every single one of God's children, no matter their creed or ideology or fake news posting habits—we need community such as this in our lives. It can become the Mordecai to our Esther: the constant, gentle reminder that God has made us of the world and for the world. It can become the lesson of a lifetime in what being a Christian truly, frightfully, wonderfully entails.

Hands, Feet, Body, Blood

If not now, when? And if not me, then who?

True confession: I already know the answers, God. But if I give them voice, I consign myself to living them, and I'm not sure I will ever be ready enough for that.

Please nudge me from this place of not enough. Show me I am enough. Remind me you are more than enough. Help me say the answers out loud and live them even louder.

Amen.

Easy

How easy to give up.

How easy to ignore. Excuse. Hide.

How easy to claim no responsibility, to throw up my hands against the avalanching world and run, knowing that my puny frame is no match for its force.

How easy. Much easier than the hard work of staying. Much easier than the hard work of contributing. Much easier than the hard work of educating myself and others, confronting tragedy and injustice, and challenging my beliefs and faith.

How easy to give up.

Easier still to never start.

To the God who knows my hesitation: push me, trip me, do whatever you need to do to move me forward, as long as I'm not just standing here.

Amen.

To be, or not to be, that is the question—
Whether 'tis Nobler in the mind to suffer
The Slings and Arrows of outrageous Fortune,
Or to take Arms against a Sea of troubles,
And by opposing end them?
                          —William Shakespeare, *Hamlet*

Take Arms

When the wrenching events of the day scratch our eyes and
claw our hearts, let us not stick our heads in the nearest
sandbox, but rather name, decry, and challenge the red-eyed
horse galloping across our floating rock, drumming its
thunderous hooves against the shrinking grass.

Let us devote our flash-in-the-pan lives to obstructing its path
and making it question—if only for a snorting, sweating
second—if it would do better to halt. For in that second we
have hope, and in that second the grass transforms to steel.

Amen.

Everywhere, Light

We've crossed the threshold once again where the sapphire night is deepest. But from this moment on, the day will fight back. Stand taller. Regain its ground.

All of us around the world, in our own times and ways, fight this battle. And we all choose the same weapon: light. Flickering, sputtering, winking, burning light. Pure in its creation. Honest in its stance. Holy in the way it reveals our path.

Amen.

What Happened When I Crossed the Bridge to Selma

The bridge leading into Selma, Alabama, arcs across the Alabama River, the central span its most decorative flourish on an
otherwise basic design. Its name: the Edmund Pettus Bridge.
Also US-80.

I never thought I'd see this bridge in person, yet here I was
as part of an unexpected day trip with a local friend I was visiting. I recognized it from textbooks and documentaries, the
background for determined civil rights activists facing off
against helmeted state troopers in the Deep South. I remembered a future Georgia congressman was among the marchers.
I knew the demonstration had turned violent and that U2 had
written a song that vaguely touched on it. I thought that the
bridge would be bigger, as I suppose of so many historical land-
marks when I encounter them without cropping or voiceovers.

The area around the bridge didn't seem to match its significance. On one side was a series of abandoned and run-down
strip malls, hodgepodge memorials, and a Voting Rights
Museum that appeared closed. On the other was historic Selma,
a pretty little downtown that at first seemed quaint until I realized the main drag was empty despite it being a sunny spring
Saturday. The entire scene felt like it was grasping, almost
desperate.

The disconnect gnawed at me. Where was the uplift? Where
was the dream fulfilled, the redemption story I'd been taught
every February during our Black History Month curriculum
when I and my majority white classmates learned about a struggle that we thought had ended two decades before we were
born? I was as desperate as the boarded-up shops waiting for
tourist dollars. I wanted that bridge to sing to me. I craved a
sign that it had all come out okay, that the struggle and blood-
shed had been worth it. Instead, the town seemed thwarted.
Hopeless.

I stood along the river walk and looked at the bridge from
afar. Such a generic span, without the technical wonder of the

Brooklyn Bridge or the evocative grandeur of the Golden Gate. Yet I was drawn to it in a way I'd never been drawn to those other places. It forced uncomfortable questions on me: "Would you have marched across me? Would you have traveled to join the protesters? Or would you have turned off the TV?"

In theory I can put myself on the side of right, but values and courage aren't always so easy to muster. Taking a stand requires work, moxie, and Teflon skin. You have to endure hurt and heartache and hope that your investment amounts to something meaningful in the end.

I want to be someone who marches across the bridge. I want to accept that maybe justice won't prevail and then fight for it anyway. I want to participate, not spectate. Is this urge half the battle? Is it enough to get me at least to the edge?

I never thought I'd see the bridge to Selma in person. I never expected even to be in Selma. But I'm glad I was, because it took being there for me to grasp what my teachers had been trying to drum into my head during all those February lessons: conviction is nothing without action.

On the Bridge

A bridge is not a conveyor belt. It will not roll beneath my feet or glide me forward. It will enable me to get from point A to point B, but it is not responsible for the getting.

Help me get to getting, God. Move my feet, leaden with fear. March me toward right, and stand with me in the crossing.

Amen.

Power without love is reckless and abusive, and love without power is sentimental and anemic. Power at its best is love implementing the demands of justice, and justice at its best is power correcting everything that stands against love.

> —Rev. Dr. Martin Luther King, Jr.,
> *The Autobiography of Martin Luther King, Jr.*

A Vein of Iron

God, give my love a vein of iron
so that my choices open gates instead of locking bars,
so that my shoulders can support the heft of justice,
so that I am solid enough to push through,
weighted enough to bear wisdom,
and substantial enough to wield the full power
of love's transforming potential.

Amen.

Make a Dent

God, protect the dent-makers. Inspire the instigators, rally the rabble-rousers, carry the catalysts.

Plant in them a conscience and the will to follow it.

Instill in them compassion to hear and respect the other side.

Help them play nice with others while defending the sandbox.

Give them plenty of space across their towns, along their blocks, and in their hearts to accommodate expansion.

And if they don't yet think they are dent-makers—or don't believe they can be—open their eyes to what they most care about, and then appear in the sightline to remind them they're not alone.

Amen.

Liberty means responsibility. That is why most men dread
it.

—George Bernard Shaw

Go-Getter

God of the get-up-and-go, give us proactive spirits. Show us
how to grip our lives with two hands and shake them up
when they need shaking.

Propel us forward on paths that serve your glory. Remind us
that our limits are imagined, for in your eyes scale loses
meaning, and meaning scales.

Above all, help us remember that whatever we act on, tiny or
tremendous, the world is not the same once the moment
passes, and we are not the same for having acted.

Amen.

Don't Forget to Hope

I'd started addressing the subject of hopefulness in talks to small groups. I'd grown fond of quoting Vaclav Havel, the great Czech leader who had said that "hope" was the one thing that people struggling in Eastern Europe needed during the era of Soviet domination.

Havel had said that people struggling for independence wanted money and recognition from other countries; they wanted more criticism of the Soviet empire from the West and more diplomatic pressure. But Havel had said that these were things they wanted; the only thing they needed was hope. Not that pie in the sky stuff, not a preference for optimism over pessimism, but rather an "orientation of the spirit." The kind of hope that creates a willingness to position oneself in a hopeless place and be a witness, that allows one to believe in a better future, even in the face of abusive power. That kind of hope makes one strong.
—Bryan Stevenson, *Just Mercy*

How easy, when current events bear sinister echoes of the past, to forget that history can and will repeat itself, if we let it.

How easy, when we finally awaken to the systemic violence and injustice our world is built on, to forget that everyone always has a choice.

How easy, when winter buffets our bodies and souls with blustery phlegm, to forget that we have soil, seeds, and the opportunity to plant in spring.

In the face of the world's overwhelming trauma, indignity, aggression, injustice, inequality—to say nothing of fate's mere caprice—it's hard to believe I can change things. Harder still to choose action. Hardest yet to imagine a future powered by hope.

But hope really is the perfect fuel for imagination because it favors abundance over scarcity and joy over despair. With hope, the future becomes an expansive frontier instead of a daunting abyss. And in glimpsing what's possible, I become even more invested in the outcome.

Hope alone creates this vision. How easy, then, to seek it.

Hope is a Weed

Hope is a stubborn weed I pull with all my strength and never kill. Roots yanked, stems crushed, ground poisoned, hope rises to defy its fate. Not only rises, but twists, snakes, worms its way around the two-layer fence I erected against all menacing threats. Not only breaches the fence, but reaches the complacent beds I was certain I'd protected. Not only reaches them, but digs in deep. Real deep. Center-of-the-earth deep. So deep, in fact, that it creeps back through the soil to the sun and all the while laughs—laughs!—at my misplaced effort in a wild, unruly world.

Give me more weeds, God of hope. Overgrow my heart to choke out fear.

Amen.

EIGHT

Courage: You Want Me to Do What?

The Scared Person's Guide to Bravery

> You may be disappointed if you fail, but you are doomed if you don't try.
>
> —Beverly Sills

What, exactly, is bravery?

It's often painted in militaristic terms—rooftop proclamations, flags planted in triumph, bellowing brute force. But braver still is a handshake: an overture to peace.

To be brave is to defy self-preservation. It dares the uncomfortable and invites the pain. Bravery accepts what must be done and does it when no one else is bothering. Bravery is the pit in your stomach before the plunge and the release you feel after the thud. Bravery is appreciating the stakes. It finds glory in the attempt, not in the victory.

Who's to say what victory is, anyway? Maybe in this moment being brave is victory enough. If so, acknowledge it. Bravery doesn't sneer or gloat, but it does permit itself a laugh, a sigh, and an occasional pat on a back.

Bravery is getting going. Bravery is stopping. Bravery is trying at all. It's knowing you did what you thought was right, even when right is murky. Bravery is demonstrated. It starts hard conversations. It signs its letters. It makes eye contact. Most importantly it listens, boldly, unabashedly, to the God voice that whispers through intuition, gut instinct, conscience—tuning in to what must come next.

Bravery requires much and often returns less. Yet I ask to be brave, because bravery is the only way any real work gets done.

Bull's-Eye

Bravery is not shooting the arrow. Bravery is being the target. Put me square in the bull's-eye, red and blaring, from this moment on to beckon the challenge.

Amen.

And that is the wonder of all wonders, that God loves the lowly. God is not ashamed of the lowliness of human beings. God marches right in. He chooses people as his instruments and performs his wonders where one would least expect them.

—Dietrich Bonhoeffer, *God Is in the Manger: Reflections on Advent and Christmas*

Unexceptional

How commonplace my commonality, how typical my type. No great shakes am I, not even a mediocre wiggle. I came in second place in the second-rate runoff. I am so so-so that no one would bother writing home about me—just this run-of-the-mill pedestrian they passed, clichéd, unacknowledged, on the street.

What then about my undistinguished life distinguishes me to you? In your eyes I am poetry masquerading as prose. I appear as routine but in reality am radical. To you, it is unacceptable to say I am anything less than exceptional.

So how shall we together prove you right?

Amen.

The true courage is in facing danger when you are afraid, and that kind of courage you have in plenty.
> —L. Frank Baum, *The Wonderful Wizard of Oz*

If I Only Had the Nerve

Confront a coworker. Call a date. Receive criticism. Stick to a principle. Demand justice. Defend my faith.

Small or huge, such actions take grit, gumption, and courage. Ah, courage. How often I feel like the Cowardly Lion, all bravado and bluster until night falls and I wind up crying into my tail. In the end, though, the Lion stepped up when his friends needed him most. He discovered reserves of strength and dignity he previously dismissed. And such storehouses can only come from you.

Amen.

The Battle of the Whole-Hearted

I once asked a question of my Facebook friends, "How do you define vulnerability?" The answers rolled in almost immediately.

"Vulnerability is having sex with the lights on after your body has been through two pregnancies."
"It's signing a lease with a Craigslist companion and moving in with people who are virtually strangers."
"It's putting yourself out there through writing."
"It's dining alone in a restaurant."

As an adjective, "vulnerable" comes off as dire: "capable of being physically or emotionally wounded; open to attack or damage" (Merriam-Webster). Where's the incentive in that? Why ever be unguarded and exposed if the only results awaiting you involve pain and harm?

I am reminded of vulnerability's double-edged sword every time I hand over my heart to joy, wrapped only in a thin layer of half-popped bubble wrap, with nary a question of what might happen. And it's probably best I don't ask anything because the answer can include disappointment, ego bruises, full-out breaks—if also discovery, excitement, and fulfillment.

Vulnerability is not weakness. Vulnerability requires courage, vast stores of it, actually. When my little beleaguered heart forgets this and comes back to me gripping its tattered bubble wrap and looking shamefaced, I sigh, hug it, and recall the guidance of storyteller and researcher Brene Brown:

Vulnerability is the core of shame and fear and our struggle for worthiness, but it appears that it's also the birthplace of joy, of creativity, of belonging, of love. . . . You can't numb those hard feelings without numbing the other affects, our emotions. You cannot selectively numb. So when we numb those, we numb joy, we numb gratitude, we numb happiness. And then we are miserable, and we are looking for purpose and meaning, and then we feel vulnerable, so then we have a couple of beers and a banana nut muffin. And it becomes this dangerous cycle.[5]

What cruel evolutionary tactic is at work that we trade nut muffins for purpose and meaning? Why would we declare ourselves unworthy of a messy, seeking, open-hearted life? I hereby claim my right both to pints of Guinness or Ben & Jerry's and my angry drives or ugly cries when I need to. These are honest responses to real emotions. And then I will lean into my vulnerability with curiosity, humility, and gratitude for the umpteen chances it always presents me to learn, change, and grow.

At the Front Window

You never intended me to sit behind a closed, fading curtain in a musty room, peeking out at the overwhelming world only when unexpected noises interrupt my daytime television programs.

When I shout "Why?" from my careworn armchair and shake a half-hearted fist at you, keep replying "Because!" and shove my creaky bones into the human tides of the awakened street so I can see, in the bright hubbub and bustle, what you mean.

Amen.

Bolded

God of overthinking, forgive my laser-like focus on the negative, which drums up heartening zingers like these:

> What if I hurt someone?
> What if I get it wrong?
> What if I hate it?
> What if I overreact?
> What if I can't cut it?

But what if I changed my vocabulary?

> What if I help someone?
> What if I get it right?
> What if I love it?
> What if I respond?
> What if I try?

What would happen then, God? What might be? What would you make of it? Of me?

Amen.

Retread

I'm walking down a familiar path of doubt, worry, and fear. Though I know this road well, I get lost every time. The route never looks the same; trees move, shadows shift, and you're always there somewhere, just out of sight, your only hint an occasional footfall ahead.

Make yourself known, Mysterious Travel Companion. Don't bother reminding me that whenever I've trailed behind you here before, we've always made it out on the other side. In fact, just consider this fact forgotten the minute the sun sets and I'm surrounded by hooting owls and howling wolves.

Step forward. Or step harder. Step somewhere, do something—I don't know, crack a twig?—to show me that the barest whisper of you is enough to base my journey on. Because right now the idea of making my way on false pretenses is terrifying, and I don't want to misinterpret any signals you send.

I look forward to spotting the flares and hearing the whistles. Rescue helicopters also appreciated. Thank you, and please.

Amen.

Be the River?

Be the river, says my friend, by which he means go with the flow, wear down the rocks, and any other number of calm and soothing water metaphors.

He forgets rivers can rage. They freeze under winter's grip, choke on melted snow, explode in summer storms, and gasp for air in arid seasons.

I'm only the river in that I react more than I control. I don't know what rocks sit in my path or how fast the current flows or where my destination rests. At best, I reflect the sunlight when it reaches me and absorb the raindrops when they fall. And always I move forward, pulled by a force set long before I joined this earth, on a course that will persist long after I depart.

I'll be the river, God, not because I have no choice, but because you have given me power between the banks: fluid strength, coursing energy, and the ability to heal myself in time.

Amen.

Cover Me

As night lowers and dawn hovers
I thank you, most Divine of lovers,
For friendships uncovered,
Sanity recovered,
And wisdom discovered.

You make me braver.

Amen.

NINE
Creativity: What If . . . ?

"A Light, Life-Charged"

Robert had little patience with these introspective bouts of mine. He never seemed to question his artistic drives, and by his example, I understood that what matters is the work: the string of words propelled by God becoming a poem, the weave of color and graphite scrawled upon the sheet that magnifies His motion. To achieve within the work a perfect balance of faith and execution. From this state of mind comes a light, life-charged.

—Patti Smith, *Just Kids*

In Patti Smith's beautiful love letter to kindred spirit-ship, life was art was love was friendship, especially with her best friend and one-time lover Robert Mapplethorpe at her side. Together Smith and Mapplethorpe explored and experimented as artists, never judging each other unless it was to say, "You can do even better." And though Mapplethorpe in particular desired acclaim, the act of creating was their primary aim. In fact, as Smith says above, it was as if their art was "propelled by God."

The connection between spirituality and creativity has long fascinated me. In particular I wonder: Does God engender creativity, and does creativity engender God? How does God define creativity? Is all creativity a gift? If not, when is creativity not good, and do the darker shades come from God as well? What makes creativity most fruitful—free rein, or limits? Are all of us endowed with creativity? Is creativity a value? A moral? A moral obligation?

Smith writes that it's "faith and execution. . . . a light, life-charged." Faith, in that you try to do it. In that you can do it. In that you should do it. In that you want to do it—or even if you don't want to, you do it anyway. Execution, in that it comes out

close to what you envisioned. In that it comes out exactly as you
envisioned. In that it comes out as only you can envision. In that
it comes out as God envisioned—or as you envision God.

Light, in that you see it. In that you follow it. In that you
fulfill it. In that you live it—and that it lives through you.

Charged

You have imposed on me a responsibility as medium. You
command me to be a conduit, exhort me to be the exhortation.

But then you take me one step further. I become more than
the hand or brush—I'm the stroke on the canvas. I'm more
than the pen or ink—I'm the word on the page. I'm more than
the numbers or sketches—I'm the invention itself.

In the finale I'm both display and viewer, producer and patron,
the fruition of your boundless imagination. In such a
triumphant moment, who is exalting whom? Does it matter?
Perhaps that is the great truth behind your creation: that act
and actor are synonymous, and we celebrate the beauty beheld.

Amen.

In Captivity

Imagination rests in the shadowy corner of the gray cage, its many-hued chest slowly rising and falling, waiting for me to release it.

Every so often, at my bidding, it steps forth for some mundane task. But I've never unleashed it. Never challenged it. Never trusted it.

Today, God, give me the courage to let my imagination run wild. Time is not a barrier, nor is failure. When heartache comes, don't let it calcify what is boundless.

I wish for a vivid and visionary life. I wish for faith in a wild creature. I wish for an imagination that can't recall captivity.

Amen.

The Genesis of Art

In the beginning, when God created the heavens and the earth, the earth was a formless wasteland, and darkness covered the abyss, while a mighty wind swept over the waters.

Then God said, "Let there be light," and there was light. God saw how good the light was. God then separated the light from the darkness. God called the light "day," and the darkness he called "night." Thus evening came, and morning followed—the first day.

Then God said, "Let there be a dome in the middle of the waters, to separate one body of water from the other." And so it happened: God made the dome, and it separated the water above the dome from the water below it. God called the dome "the sky." Evening came, and morning followed—the second day.

Then God said, "Let the water under the sky be gathered into a single basin, so that the dry land may appear." And so it happened: the water under the sky was gathered into its basin, and the dry land appeared. God called the dry land "the earth," and the basin of the water he called "the sea." God saw how good it was. Then God said, "Let the earth bring forth vegetation: every kind of plant that bears seed and every kind of fruit tree on earth that bears fruit with its seed in it." And so it happened: the earth brought forth every kind of plant that bears seed and every kind of fruit tree on earth that bears fruit with its seed in it. God saw how good it was. Evening came, and morning followed—the third day.

Then God said: "Let there be lights in the dome of the sky, to separate day from night. Let them mark the fixed times, the days and the years, and serve as luminaries in the dome of the sky, to shed light upon the earth." And so it happened: God made the two great lights, the greater one to govern the day, and the lesser one to govern the night; and he made the stars. God set them in the dome of the sky, to shed light upon the earth, to govern the day and the night, and to separate the light from the darkness. God saw how good it was. Evening came, and morning followed—the fourth day.

Then God said, "Let the water teem with an abundance of living creatures, and on the earth let birds fly beneath the dome of the sky." And so it happened: God created the great sea monsters and all kinds of swimming creatures with which the water teems, and all kinds of winged birds. God saw how good it was, and God blessed them, saying, "Be fertile, multiply, and fill the water of the seas; and let the birds multiply on the earth." Evening came, and morning followed—the fifth day.

Then God said, "Let the earth bring forth all kinds of living creatures: cattle, creeping things, and wild animals of all kinds." And so it happened: God made all kinds of wild animals, all kinds of cattle, and all kinds of creeping things of the earth. God saw how good it was. Then God said: "Let us make man in our image, after our likeness. Let them have dominion over the fish of the sea, the birds of the air, and the cattle, and over all the wild animals and all the creatures that crawl on the ground."

God created man in his image; in the divine image he created him; male and female he created them.

God blessed them, saying: "Be fertile and multiply; fill the earth and subdue it. Have dominion over the fish of the sea, the birds of the air, and all the living things that move on the earth." God also said: "See, I give you every seed-bearing plant all over the earth and every tree that has seed-bearing fruit on it to be your food; and to all the animals of the land, all the birds of the air, and all the living creatures that crawl on the ground, I give all the green plants for food." And so it happened. God looked at everything he had made,

and he found it very good. Evening came, and morning
followed—the sixth day.

                                        —Genesis 1:1-31

By my count, we have seven elements in this biblical passage
that God deems good: light; earth and sea; vegetation; stars;
sea monsters, swimming creatures, and winged birds; wild animals, cattle, and creeping things; and humankind. Then God
steps back, surveys what they hath wrought, and deems it all
worthy. To my mind, each element represents a critical piece of
the creative process—not just for the biblical beginning but
also for the creative births that all artists midwife.

Light is the spark: the candle in the window, the sometimes
brief but vivid hint that something bigger, deeper, richer lies
ahead if we keep walking. Earth and sea form the foundations
that either stay firm beneath our feet or carry us securely in their
currents. They are our envelope: the structure that gives us a
cyclical, reliable, immutable space in which to play. Vegetation
acts as both fuel and cover. It nourishes us when our energy flags
and shelters us when our eyelids droop. Stars symbolize our
greater compass, the fiery winks that point toward meaning.
Why must this work of art live, they ask, and why are you the
one to bring it forth? Sea monsters, swimming creatures, and
winged birds reflect wild leaps, flights of fancy, the spasms of
imagination that grip us and help us to believe that what we're
making is fantastic and beautiful. Wild animals, cattle, and
creeping things ground us: they are the everyday plod, the humble crawl forward, the fight-or-flight instinct that moves us—
maybe not always in the direction we want, but that compels us
nonetheless. And then we humans, the ones gifted with imagination, ourselves the ultimate example of works in progress, dust
made animate, striving to reflect the divine through our
creativity.

In the end we look on everything we have made and experience a dizzying moment as the work takes on a very good life
independent of our own. We have no dominion over what is

created. Rather, we watch our works of art walk alone into a brave new land born of our minds, not ruled by our hands, and greater than the sum of the acts that formed them.

On the Seventh Day

On the seventh day my work will be complete.
First, a nap, and then we celebrate!
My work, however, cannot bear to rest.
Created, it must stretch, inhale, and flex,
A strut of strength within a universe
Of countless other works. Art, listen up.
Abundance is your fruit; the fact that you
Exist at all illuminates your life.
So revel mightily in your array,
Your bursting seeds, slow-creeping things, white wings
That beat against your rib cage. Multiply
At will. Dominion's overrated.

Amen.

Why Grand?

Often described as Earth's greatest geological showcase, the ensemble of stunning dimensions—the melding of depth, width, and length—sets Grand Canyon apart. Nowhere else features such a dazzling variety of colorful rock layers, impressive buttes, and shadowed side canyons. Grand Canyon is the canyon against which all other canyons are compared.... The geologic story is rich in detail and mystery. Attending a free ranger program may move you from wonder to comprehension.

> — From the "Grand Canyon Guide to
> the South Rim" pamphlet

"From Wonder to Comprehension"

How big was the easel that held your canvas for the world?

How much did you hem and haw, brush and oils in hand, while billions of years passed below? And when you formed the sun and moon, was it with an eye to the variable light they'd cast on your masterpiece?

You are the only artist I've encountered whose tools move independently. Your masterwork will never hang complete, for the natural world you set in motion edits, shapes, and evolves the art within.

I try my best to record each shifting view. Still, many I miss. Many more I've not had a chance to see. But you don't mind; instead, you wave and call me closer. There are no ropes or lines or alarms here—simply an open invitation to press my nose against the picture until I pass into the paint itself.

Amen.

Paint Chip

What do I look like in every separate light? What flatters me, flattens me? Do I change tints? Appear darker or brighter? Am I warm or cool? Am I what you expected me to be?

God, add me to your cosmic palette. Fling me Pollock-like toward the sunset—a magnificent, impermanent streak in the firmament. Treat me as a rough sketch worth revising and repainting. I will never look the same way twice, but that is precisely your vision.

Amen.

Blank Slate

I won't believe the blank slate. Instead, I'll draw a handle and turn it to reveal the swirl of watercolors beyond, looping and dipping in a hue-soaked landscape that would make Georgia O'Keeffe drool. I will draw strange birds that swoop like dragons, huge fish that dart like the Perseids, friendly trees that trundle behind me so I never want for shade. With each invention I draw, you will be both chalk and hand, the spark behind the inspiration, the spirit within the artist. May I embody your rioting symphony of shapes and shades and with them paint a world not yet envisioned.

Amen.

I, Catulla

Many high school students give their teachers cards or scented candles at the holidays. I wrote my teachers poems. And no one amassed a larger body of my work than my high school Latin teacher, Mrs. Bender. Over the course of three years, I wrote reams of translations, essays, and parodies inspired by my Latin classes. I couldn't help myself, really. The material was so rich, my concentration so intense, that not a class went by where I wasn't inspired by a character, phrase, or technique.

It all came to a head my junior year when I took AP Latin. That's when we got to the good stuff—poetry, mainly by Horace and Catullus. Everything I loved came together in this one subject: grammar, syntax, vocabulary, scansion, meter, rhyme, imagery, humor, drama, and interpretation. The idea that ancient texts could be accessible to a modern audience fascinated me, elevating rote translation homework to high art.

At the end of the semester I compiled a little book for Mrs. Bender as a thank-you gift. Titled "I, Catulla: One Latin Student's Lasting Impressions of Catullus, Horace, and Everything in Between," the teeny volume comprised six poems, two parodies, and a parting thought. I handed it over to her with great contentment, waved goodbye, and forgot about it.

Cut to 13 years later, when I took a poetry course as part of my graduate writing program. As I pored over our English texts, scribbled notes in the margins, and tapped out iambic pentameter on my thigh, I felt a familiar stirring. Suddenly I was back in the small classroom overlooking the courtyard at my high school, scanning sentences on the board, parsing passages on thematic as well as molecular levels. I heard pencils scratching, loafers scuffing, girls giggling. It was then that I remembered my little book of poems.

On a whim, I emailed Mrs. Bender and asked if, by any chance, she had kept my gift to her. A week later I received a fat envelope in the mail that contained a photocopy of every special piece I'd ever written for her, from a national award-winning translation to a Christmas poem not even connected to our class. The collection reminded me how far my imagination could reach, and how invigorated I felt when it stretched. Right on top of the stack was a standalone poem I did not remember writing—a translation of Horace Odes III.30 with the end line of I.1 tacked on for emphasis. Here's how it read:

> I have finished a steadfast monument
> more enduring than bronze, and loftier
> than regal tips of royal pyramids.
> Neither erosive rain nor winds, north-sent,
> destroy it, nor can the raging warrior
> of countless years—the flight of time—corrode.
> I will not—cannot!—die entirely,
> for much of me avoids mortal demise.
> Instead, my words (and thus my soul) will thrive,
> made fresh with future praise as long as he
> who worships questions gods within their skies.
> I will be sung as one still much alive;
> though rustic people heralded my birth,
> the royal lines exalt my lasting fame.
> O Muse, gain from my achievement rich pride,
> and willingly fashion of Delphic earth
> a laurel crown befitting my great name!
>
> For I will strike the stars, my head held high.
> —Horace Odes III.30, I.1; trans. Julia Rocchi

I read it once. I read it again. I sat with it in my hands, looking at the undated paper, repeating the words, wondering if I had not just written this the other day and somehow slipped it in the pile. Here was a work I composed when I was 16 years old, based on literature two millennia older than that, and yet the theme and voice and construction felt as familiar and fresh to me as notes I'd jotted yesterday. There was the iambic pentameter I love to scan. There was the rhyme I thrill to include.

There was the artist's statement I constantly refine. And, most telling, there was the fervent, desperate hope that the work would outshine and outlive me.

In this printout I first produced on my parents' desktop computer, I saw my entire essence as a writer foretold. Long before I found the words to express my drive, I heard a kindred spirit echoing across dusty centuries and strove to reply in rhythm and verse. If that wasn't a sign I was on the right path, what is?

Human Declension

To the Great Translator:

On accusative days, I'm acted on by others, in that they direct and I object.

On dative days, I'm more willing to receive, in that they direct and I accept.

On nominative days, I am a subject all my own—the lead, the actor, the one who calls the shots.

On ablative days, I become the means—not the doer, not the deed, but the way.

On genitive days, I simply am possessed.

But to you, I remain in vocative—a call, a cry, a name that disappears in the wind and leaves its intonation behind. You capture my substance and my essence. You convey my meaning. You change me in form but not in ending. For when my piece concludes, your translation will persist, and the final work is not yet one I know.

Amen.

Write like the self you hide and can't convey when you're speaking.

—Matthea Harvey

The Self I Hide

Help me write like the self I hide,
The part of me that steeps in shame
Or cheers, elated, at moments
Captured fully in a writer's sights.

Help me write like the self I fear,
The part of me too terrified
To fall in love with what I love
So deep I'll lose my sense of "should."

Help me write like the self I want,
The part of me that longs for blurbs
And prizes, yes, but more the part
That craves transcendence over all.

Amen.

"Tell Us in Your Own Words"

There's a delightful moment in the musical *Guys and Dolls* when self-righteous missionary General Cartwright declaims in operatic tones to gangster Nicely-Nicely Johnson, "Tell us in your own words." She's referring to the personal story of salvation he's purporting to have, and "tell us" is exactly what Nicely proceeds to do, not just with words, but with rhyme, rhythm, melody, harmony, and a full choreographed dance routine alongside a bunch of sin-riddled gamblers.

Could the character have stated his story simply, *à la* group therapy? Sure. But this being a Broadway musical, he was beholden by the laws of his theatrical universe to make it big. Different. Memorable. So memorable, in fact, that twenty years after I first listened to the *Guys and Dolls* revival cast recording in my parents' car, I can still recite "Sit Down, You're Rocking the Boat" by heart.

I once channeled a bit of General Cartwright when a poet friend shared how unhappy she'd become with her verse. "I want to be like Robert Frost," she told me. "He has these perfect images, and he just drops this wisdom in, but everything I write comes out coy or arch."

"Is that your voice, though? What if instead of fighting it, you embraced it?"

She considered that for half a second. "But I don't like it. I want to be like Frost."

I tried again. "But why be a second Frost when you can be a first you? I want to hear your voice. What do you have to say?"

She was having none of it. Which means, to my great sorrow, that I will have none of her for the foreseeable future. None of her wit, none of her creativity, none of her singular view of the world.

What do I have if not my own voice? Who else has my exact senses and sensibilities? Who else has my mix of experiences, my list of desires, my raft of dreams? No one. Only me. For you, only you.

Two roads diverged in a wood, and I—
I took the one less traveled by
And that has made all the difference

I doubt the poet who gave us these classic lines would want a writer to follow his well-trod path. Let's plot our own instead and explore a wilderness uncharted.

My Own Course

Rock your own boat. Plow your own field. Tilt at your own windmills, the ones whose steady thrums claim you cannot defeat them.

God of voice and character, speak through the conflicted cacophony in my own mind. Endow what I have to say with confidence. Help me leave my windmills far in my past, twirling listlessly against an empty sky, while I carry my message farther than I believed possible.

Amen.

A Plot Afoot

In the beginning, I feared the end.

In the middle, I worried I hadn't begun.

In the end, I wondered why I'd wasted energy fearing and worrying when instead I could have enjoyed the beginning and the middle.

God, help me live each act as it comes and turn the pages at just the right pace.

Amen.

Alas for those that never sing,
But die with all their music in them!
                                    —Oliver Wendell Holmes

Yes, Music Is the Food of Love

Play on, play on, all you musical creatures
With voices and strings and other fine features
That vibrate our souls in ethereal chords
And speak of vast worlds that live beyond words.

Play on, all you gifted with joy in your hearts,
And teach those you meet their harmonious parts.
Music, like fire, has graced us since dawn,
And like water or blood, we know it flows on.

For music is heard in our joints and our bones,
Our minds and our eyes—not just ears alone.
Thus no one is tone deaf, and all are musicians
When they play among life's symphonic procession.

So gorge on love's food and gulp down its wine;
Savor each bite, for it's wholly divine.
God gave us our songs not to swallow but sing—
Throw back your heads and play your heartstrings.

Amen.

Pitch Imperfect

Siren singing on a distant baby grand
I am power
I am motion
I am jazz and smoke and a very late night . . .

Then I wake up, away from a stage, with a hummingbird trill, a sunny outlook, and a dimple I didn't know I had.

What have you made me? What will you make me? Are these two selves—present and future, inner and outer—necessarily opposites? Or are they refractions, evidence of your endless permutations, and a promise of constant re-interpretation?

Amen.

Rustic

Rough, plain, simple are we, unfinished yet sturdy in our make. Master Carpenter who chisels each of us with vibrant hand, eschew all formal plans and help us embrace our wild forms. By your grace alone, our spirits refine our raw materials, proving that we do not need perfection to be loved.

Amen.

Conviction Set in Concrete

I've been inside umpteen churches, toured many magnificent cathedrals, but not until I visited the Basilica de la Sagrada Familia in Barcelona did I feel so connected to humanity, nature, and divinity. Its vivid colors, nurturing curves, symbology and storytelling in every nook—Gaudí's vision was Catholic and catholic simultaneously, making me feel what I too often only think about.

Part of the power of the Sagrada experience was standing in a work in progress. Most churches I've visited are ancient and settled. But Sagrada was surrounded by cranes and scaffolding. The inside was only completed and consecrated by Pope Benedict in 2010, and total completion isn't expected until after 2026. (Or, as the tour guide's joke went, "between now and eventually.")

It staggers me to consider that even with modern technologies and capabilities, it has taken more than 150 years to build this temple of God. And that I was part of that flow of time, at least for an afternoon. I bore witness to the scope and intimacy of Gaudí's creative plans. He accounted for every inch, bringing to bear all his skills in architecture, engineering, sculpture, masonry, coppersmithing, woodworking, and storytelling. He laid out meticulous plans, knowing he would not live to see the cathedral to completion, instead trusting others to finish it. I wonder if he was sad to miss it, or comforted knowing it would live beyond him, or maybe both.

The exhibit panels inside the Basilica told me that Gaudí was a devout believer. He certainly believed in the project, and it shows. The entire building breathes around you. It moves with the earth. Despite its vastness, it doesn't dwarf but rather elevates you. A half-hearted person could not have achieved this miracle. La Sagrada Familia is conviction set in concrete.

In hectic moments since my experience there, I find my mind wandering back to the sanctuary. Tourists and pilgrims fade at the periphery into quiet wraiths. My eyes linger on the incomplete stained glass. The crescendo of the sung Lord's Prayer bounces off the curves. I sit in a pew and watch sunlight chart its course through dusk. It's just as Gaudí designed it, so that neither too much dark nor too much light would render the worshiper blind.

It's a temple built for rejoicing. It metes no punishment and wags no fingers. It doesn't seek to smother with grandeur. It's there to guide, instruct, and exclaim. La Sagrada Familia was built with palms open and eyes up. It can't stop smiling. No wonder I felt overjoyed in the moment and continue to experience its reverberations today.

Someday, I hope to return with my children or grandchildren and stand amid a forest of pillars beneath a choir of a thousand singers within a church built as a prayer. I will tell my own holy family, "I was first here when this fully wasn't." It is then we will feel creativity living and breathing around us, never fixed, but alive in the dappled light.

Scaffold

My sanctuary is incomplete. I spot chinks of sunlight where ladders meet rails and shadows where hefty cranes loom overhead. I thought I had a plan when I started building. The more I construct, though, the fuzzier my blueprints become. Watchful statues ask tough questions, and higher towers bring deeper thought.

Strangely, I'm not worried. There is no rush, only unrealistic expectations. I will one day arrive at the altar, the pillars will rise piece by piece, and as long as I'm striving for beauty, I know the result will be nothing less than holy.

The unstained windows wink. They see what's coming.

Amen.

What Happens When a Dream Catches Up with You

There he was: Avi, the one-named author of more than 70 books for children and young adults, whose massive output includes *The True Confessions of Charlotte Doyle*, one of the novels that inspired me to become a writer. He was standing right there, being friendly, normal, and impossibly human. I couldn't breathe. And while I was busy not breathing—instead reliving the many hours I spent with Charlotte Doyle wondering how I could make that same magic happen across sheets of paper—the tent filled with other word nerds of all ages who had flocked to the National Book Festival that weekend to celebrate storytelling.

From the edge of my seat I watched child after child crowd the microphone, eager to ask Avi their burning questions: What inspires your characters? How do you do your research? How many drafts do you write? What's your favorite part of writing? Have you ever run into any legal problems? (Actual question.)

Avi was splendid with them—always interested, never condescending, and clear and direct with all his responses. He respected every child first as themselves, second as his readers, and third as his "potential competition" in another few years.

As Avi shared his wit and wisdom with the overflowing tent, I welled up. "Oh my god," I realized. "I can do this. This is a thing. And it's my thing. I can write and tell stories and touch people's hearts and talk to them and encourage them to do the same. I want this to be my life. This should be my life."

The conviction behind the thought overwhelmed me. I wasn't considering my day job or personal development. I wasn't project-managing the situation. I was simply stating what I wanted more deeply than anything else in the world.

The moment left me breathless. In the span of a second, I had marching orders. I didn't know where or how to march, and frankly, I was not even sure how to figure it out. It struck me that an appropriate first step would be to write something awesome that only I could write. An appropriate second step would be to get it published before I die. Beyond that, I realized I would have to make it up as I went along.

So what then? What did I do after crying at Avi? All I had was a vision of me standing in a tent on the National Mall someday, speaking with children about books, imagination, and why stories matter. But that was and is enough. Because that's what happens when a dream catches up with you in Technicolor HD 3D Smell-o-Vision. You jump between wild hope and abject terror. You try to discern which questions are worth answering first, later, or never. You fend off the pitchfork-wielding self-doubt just long enough to get the job done. You believe the dream in your heart, and then you keep believing it.

Vision (Part I)

You have planted this vision in my heart, and it is meant for me alone.

I will rail against you in frustrated moments. I will shove you aside in short-sighted weakness. I will question your judgment, my judgment, everyone's judgment, and I'll wonder why I'm sticking to a plan I can neither see nor understand.

Through all this you promise: the vision is mine and mine alone.

Because when I succeed—when I pick the lock of the hidden chamber where you stacked my nascent abilities, the same hideaway where I stowed my wildest dreams for safekeeping—then I will thank you for revealing to me early on not my results, but my potential.

Amen.

Vision (Part II)

I now grasp the vision you planted in my heart, and the view is breathtaking.

I want it more than anything I've ever wanted before. I see the lifelong potential waiting patiently in the corner, and I think I am close enough to touch it. But when I reach out, it is still one arm's length too far.

Only one, though. Closer than when it first emerged in a shadowy corner, soft and unformed at its edges, and much closer than when it snoozed alone in the dark, hidden and unknown to me. (Though you always knew it was there.)

This you promise me: you will help me do everything in my power to make up that final length. Whether I need longer arms or wider steps or 17 revolutions around the room, you will support me as I shorten the distance, just as you have supported me year after year, day after day, as I've inched closer.

Stay strong. Stay focused. Stay the course, you say. Though I might not hear it, you are cheering for me—ever louder, ever prouder.

Amen.

Vision (Part III)

I am living the vision you planted in my heart, and my awe overwhelms me.

My two minds on the matter—doubt that the vision could materialize, conviction that it would—have receded in favor of pure gratitude. Gratitude for endurance and patience, doggedness and dumb luck, constraint and inspiration. Gratitude for all the support I've received and time I've invested. Gratitude for belief in myself, in you, and in our unfolding vision.

This you promise me: As much as I am celebrating right now, you are celebrating me a hundredfold. You have always celebrated me, in fact, because you love me for who I am, not what I do.

Yes, I have coaxed a conflagration from a single spark, a feat worthy of appreciation. But the true miracle is witnessing my formation as it happens. I will rejoice in this gift and see what new vision it creates.

Amen.

The Writer's Worst Enemy

I sat in the coffee shop yesterday, laptop at hand, with one goal: write a new picture book manuscript in two hours.

The cursor blinked but for a moment. I knew exactly what I wanted to say. I could read every acceptance letter from publishers, see every illustration in my head, hear every parent reading it aloud at bedtime to expectant little faces.

I clickety-clacked my heart out, undaunted by the white page, unwavering in my self-belief. I had no reason to hesitate. I knew this was pure gold.

Until I read what I'd written.

That's when I realized: Blank pages are not the enemies writers make them out to be. First drafts are.

Blank pages are the easy part. They're shining beacons of potential and hope. I haven't offended anyone with bad grammar or struggled to fill a plot hole or dyed the whole thing red with editorial ink. Blank pages hold only my best intentions.

First drafts, however, reveal just how far I am from my initial, glorious vision. All the work's imperfections have emerged in harsh sunlight with bad hangovers. Characters trip over each other and lose their voices. Chapters drag like mummy feet. The text is pretentious on one page, trite on another, and for the love of God, do not. Put in. That epilogue.

Coming up short is scary. *Wait, I wasn't perfect out of the gate?* I think. It shakes my confidence. Better the page remain blank and be imagined perfect than to fill it up and inject all doubt.

Where does this leave us, besides crying in the corner and taking to drink? As I see it, we have two options for our work:

1. Put on blinders. Insist on your consummate brilliance. Consider your job done.
2. Admit your weaknesses. Admit your strengths. Keep working.

How like life writing can be. The most productive route usually isn't the easiest. Or the fastest. Or the cleanest. I sat reading that picture book draft and watched my happy day-dreams evaporate like the steam off the espresso machine. But I knew they'd coalesce again soon, because the visions, goals, and ambitions are cyclical. I don't diminish or abandon them. I just set them alongside the first draft to keep a watchful eye on my progress. The worst part is over. I have put real words on paper. Now I have something to work with. Something to improve. To relish. To earn.

Work in Progress

God of sparks and daydreams and notebook doodles—

Take what is passable and elevate it.
Take what is useable and sculpt it.
Take what is good and burnish it.

Make me superlative, just as you envisioned.

Amen.

When Competition Defeats Me

To be a writer is to invite defeat. Defeat in competitions, in publications, in the will and drive to continue. I know because I set a goal to receive 100 rejections in one calendar year, and I am already feeling black and blue at a measly 13 and wondering if I should invest in a more robust liquor cabinet to get through the year.

The hurt stems not only from rejections, either. I feel the sting every time a fellow writer announces a publication or a fellowship, an article or an award. It doesn't matter if they're short story writers like I am or science/medical scribes appearing in peer-reviewed journals to which I have never aspired. The punch lands on my jaw all the same because they, at least on the face of it, have what I want: recognition that their art has merit.

In my deepest moments of self-pity, I regard myself as a Rock 'Em Sock 'Em robot of futility—a blank figurine pinned within a ring I wonder why I asked to enter, caught unaware when the next slug connects and my head pops off my shoulders. But after my head drops back and I pause to observe my plastic prison, I see it's not that intimidating. Only a flimsy rope keeps me from the wider, woolly world—the very world I say I want yet am scared to inhabit.

The true villain, then, is my fear. Fear of being outpaced and outclassed. Fear of overestimating my potential. Fear of not leaving a faint smudge of immortality somewhere in the notebook of human civilization.

Look at how cheaply the rope is made, though, how artificial its construct. On closer examination, I start to see what sets me apart from the Red Rocker or Blue Bomber. Unlike them, I have agency. No one is pushing joysticks beneath me; I can stand there and jab at unfeeling air, or I can leave the ring to try punching above my weight.

I'm considering these words of wisdom from fiction author Colum McCann:

If you're writing to beat someone else then you're writing with invisible ink. Watch it disappear. Instead keep counsel with dignity. . . . This does not mean that you don't want to be better than another writer—being better is part of the job. But be better in a better way. In a way that hurts. In a way that forces you into competition with yourself. If you're going to throw a punch try your own jaw first.[6]

With 87 rejections ahead of me, I am not aiming to win faster. I am vowing to fight harder.

Rope-a-Dope

Lay me flatter than my own low standards. Launch me higher than my timid goals. When I'm on the ropes, shove me through them, and when I hit the floor on the other side, expectorated into a new and limitless arena, raise my arm in jubilant victory, for I will have already vanquished the toughest opponents I will ever face.

Amen.

Culmination

More could be said. More could be tweaked. More could be sliced and diced and reimagined ad infinitum. But eventually, your vision must toddle forth on its own two legs. You have to trust what guided it to this point. You need to believe in your own ability and stand by what you sought to create.

God, grant us the right kind of pride—satisfied, elated, self-respecting. Work well done is work worth celebrating. Help us honor it now.

Amen.

TEN

Joy: God, Do You Laugh?

The Radical Rebellion

"Does God laugh?"

My friend's 4-year-old daughter once posed this question to her. As my friend later explained in a Facebook post, the question led to a "rather profound inquiry into what sort of things God would and wouldn't laugh at. One of the clear distinctions [my daughter] made was that God laughs with people, not at people. Also, God likes it when we're being silly."

No wonder my friend called her daughter a little theologian. With a simple three-word question the child hit on a deep truth about God that we harried, stressed adults too often forget: God created us with joy, from joy, for joy.

C.S. Lewis touched on a similar theme in his book *Letters to Malcolm, Chiefly on Prayer* when he wrote, "Joy is the serious business of heaven." God did not create a world of pain and suffering and then say, "You know what? I'm going to stick some humans in here and watch them squirm." Rather, God created paradise—an exuberant playground, a world designed to delight. We have voices to sing, hands to clap, feet to dance, hearts to leap, and Thin Mints to devour. What's not to love?

What I have learned, however, is that joy is not necessarily a given in our lives. The more we slip into easy pessimism, the more joy becomes a choice. The distinction crystallizes for me in this translation of Romans 5:11 from the King James Version of the Bible: "And not only so, but we also joy in God through our Lord Jesus Christ, by whom we have now received the atonement." We joy in God. Joy as vivifying verb. Joy as animating action. Joy as intentional summons from a gift we've already received yet have forgotten.

Henri Nouwen spoke to the need to activate this gift when he wrote, "Joy does not simply happen to us. We have to choose joy and keep choosing it every day." The choice becomes easier once I remember joy's effects. Just the mental image of God laughing fills me with a lightness and peace. Imagine how a life lived with constant joy would affect others around me. To choose joy is to rebel against cynicism and meanness. To choose joy is radical.

May all our wild actions be born of belly laughter, slow-spreading smiles, and astonished gasps. May we come to know the profound comfort of laughing with the God we enchant.

Silly for Joy

God of heel clicks and high fives, keep me so silly for joy that I can't see straight.

When I am downtrodden, joy props me up.

When I am flattened, joy re-inflates me.

When I am beaten, joy wipes my brow and hands me water.

When I am proud, joy grounds me in wonder bigger than myself.

When I am uncertain, joy reminds me I am worthy.

And when all I am is joyful, joy cheers loudest of all.

Amen.

The Good Terror

I have termed it "the good terror"—when your chest is splayed open to the world and your heart tha-THUMP-tha-THUMPs in broad daylight, unprotected and unguarded from all the joy flying at it. Good because joy carries abundance and wakes you up laughing. Terror because joy can frighten a body, especially when it piles high enough to invite distrust.

In what has been the happiest month yet in a miserable year, I'm trying to embrace the contradiction, and through these feeble attempts I have rediscovered small joys that slipped through the cracks in bluer times. Openheartedness brought me back to cheese and crackers. Flouncy clothes over a warm summer tan. A homemade mix CD right before dream time. Openheartedness prompted me to write a prayer with a gel pen on college-ruled paper. Dance to *Sam Cooke: Live at the Harlem Square Club* before an evening out on the town. Not turn on the stove all weekend and eat caprese salad for two consecutive meals. Joy, I remembered, is singing alongside a drum circle and holding hands during church. It's affirming a kindred spirit over a Sunday morning strata. It's that incredulous, grateful lurch in the pit of your stomach when your lover moves in to kiss you.

The good terror doesn't need an invitation. It doesn't even need a reason. Just a yes. The joy will take it from there.

Resting in the Joy

Sitting in the happy, resting in the joy,
Taking just a minute to bask and loll within it
And appreciate the sunlight unalloyed.

Asking not "Why me?" Saying "Yes, let's!"
Welcome respite, this, to saturate with bliss—
The kind of gift one never gives, but gets.

Amen.

Today was my grandmother's birthday, so to celebrate, she and my grandfather went to look at their gravesites, and then they went to Olive Garden.

—my friend Jacob

For Good Reason

Uncork that special bottle of wine, for what's worth celebrating more than this moment in time?

Join me on the dance floor, shoes tossed under the rented table, so we can sway offbeat.

Hold my hand on a stroll through a darkening town this late summer night.

Wing a postcard (or seven) across the miles to include me in your adventure.

Tee-hee with me behind a cupped hand and keep my happy secrets forever.

Thank you for the breathtaking reminder that my days here, though limited, run deep. And though it may be more joy than I can take, I also ask you this: Dive into the glimmering pool with me. Take me leagues beyond what I feel today. May we never reach the horizon.

Amen.

Laff Track

Joy walks in on laughter's back; humor invites them both. Thank you for switching on lights in forgotten rooms and reminding me that laughter likes to hide—and be discovered—in unexpected places.

Amen.

Saturated

When one's cup runneths over, where does it spill? Can I scoop the excess in a spare glass, stick it in the fridge, and use it later to water the plants or make a nice chicken stock?

I ask because you don't seem like the type of deity who would want good joy to go to waste. So many people's cups have leaks; who am I to hoard a bucket's worth?

I'd like to propose a reuse program, God. When my cup is runnething over, I will first thank you for all the good things you put in it. Then I will drink the cup so all that love and comfort and worthiness is sloshing inside me. Then, fortified, I will pour the runneth-off into other people's empty mugs.

In this way we'll eliminate waste and inefficiency and get that joy where it needs to be—in the hands and hearts of people who need it.

Thoughts? Suggestions? Endorsement?

Amen.

Let unconquerable gladness dwell.
>   —a motto of Franklin Delano Roosevelt, from
>   *A Prayer Book for Soldiers and Sailors*

Unconquerable

May we draw strength from quiet victories in routine days.
May we relish the unexpected joys that shape satisfying
moments.
May we celebrate achieving our visions—and then set new
goals.
May we listen with intent to understand, and with
understanding, act.
May we take the right kind of pride in doing right by you and
by ourselves.
May we underpin our power with humility and gratitude.
May our unconquerable gladness be wrapped in you.

Amen.

In Good Times

I don't trust the good times. They're too special. Too comfortable. Too reassuring. Too good, in fact, to be true. I'd rather live through the bad times. Then at least I'm not sitting around waiting for my certain demise.

But I want to have faith in the good times, God. I want to have faith that joy is an undercurrent, not a darting ripple. I want to have faith that when hiccups, bumps, and roadblocks come again (because they will), they will not crowd out happiness but coexist with it. Not erase it, but illuminate it.

Help me invite all times and ways and feelings, God, so that I come to understand the fullness of my humanity.

Amen.

What Do You Pray for When Life is Good?

What do you pray for when the rain is dripping off the shop window mere inches from your chin cupped in your hand—a glass raincoat with a cozy, caffeinated lining?

What do you pray for when you choose paper over screens—soft pages at your fingertips, old glue scent in your nose, a world unfurling in your mind that's invisible to those passing by?

What do you pray for when the quiet murmur of a warm Saturday twilight carries you, alone save for the cuddling breeze, to dreamland on the deck?

What do you pray for when you pluck herbs from the rooftop garden and stick them in jars to perfume the kitchen you haven't gotten around to cleaning?

What do you pray for when the job is well done, and you're the one who did it, and while you have not moved mountains, you have at least nudged your own hesitant land mass a couple inches to the left?

What do you pray for when your lower register is shot because you stopped caring who heard you belt?

What do you pray for when you catch your eyelashes casting shadows on a gallery wall—a fleeting installation meant only for you?

What do you pray for when you know in your heart that good is all around you, that still more good things are coming, and that, for a brief and wondrous moment, you're patient enough to wait for them?

The Good Enough Life

My future is uncertain. My times are scary. My life is fluctuating. My mind and hours are occupied.

Yet my moments are crystallized. Perfect prisms hanging in an open window, bowing to the elements, banging against the glass but never flying off.

Keep me attached to these refractive moments; they glimmer with peace.

Amen.

The Wonder Year

Put stars in my eyes and springs under my feet. Turn my specs the deepest shade of rose. Knock me silly, gift me giddy. Let me marvel. Let me stare. Let me love unabashed what you have given me.

When I stray too close to the naysayers, push me behind you and block the path. When I drift too far from the exclaimers, sling me back into their orbit. And when I glimpse the universe in all its bigness, join me in my sudden, breathless laughter.

Amen.

Putting the Soul in Summer

Some people claim the best parties are all about the guest list, food, or open bar. I maintain they are all about the silly.

Consider my annual summer solstice party. This event goes beyond burgers and beers; it's about celebrating sunshine, relaxing without guilt, and reveling in a holiday that's not part of the summer triumvirate of Memorial Day, July 4th, and Labor Day.

The summer solstice party has a humble and innocent origin. When I was growing up in Pennsylvania, my favorite season was summer. It signaled the arrival of my birthday, pool visits, and nonstop reading. Naturally I wanted to mark this time as soon as possible, and the longest day of the year suited because we were fresh out of school and ready to blow off steam.

Each year on the day of the solstice, I'd tell all the neighborhood kids to meet me and my brother in the backyard after dinner. We'd show up in our grubby outdoor clothes and bare feet. We'd bring balls and ropes and flashlights. It was manic, magic, unbridled play. The kind of play that takes you across six backyards, helps you wear out the fireflies, and makes you run in your dreams that night.

A decade and a half later, in a new city and in a new life that didn't give me summers off or a yard to play in, I found myself wistful for my old ritual. I told my roommates about it, and we decided to resurrect the concept, this time with alcohol. The adult version was an instant hit. Even just thinking about it puts a glow in my heart and brings me right back to the original golden backyard days. It could have been that my brother was visiting me for the party, or that 70 of my closest friends showed up, or that I drank a fair amount. But I think it was our level of silly. My roommates and I had a palm tree–shaped cooler that made me chuckle every time I looked at it. Our corn muffins had cupcake wrappers with either birthday confetti or animal prints on them. We used water pistols to soak each other all throughout the evening.

Guests set off sparklers and firecrackers before it was dark. They proudly wore the glow sticks we passed around as bracelets, necklaces, and headbands. They conducted a cornhole tournament past sunset, rearranged the pink flamingos in our landscaping, and played several rounds of improv comedy in the alley.

Silly, we remembered, feels really good. It reminds us that our youngest selves—ones we thought we'd shooed away when bills in our names started arriving—still live inside us, waiting to kick off their shoes and squeal around the neighborhood. I love me some silly, and I love the season and the people who help me bring it. May I never be too old, jaded, or un-summery for any of them.

Summer Solstice

Plant grass beneath my bare soles and fly me back to the first moment I watched the long-suspended sun knit itself at last to the hazy horizon and drop new stars to earth as blinking bulbs.

In that time I was beyond wonder. I simply saw. Believed. No, knew. Return me heady and heated to that deep purple dusk where I can seek for you hiding in the landscaping, stifling a giggle.

Amen.

Wonder

Rapt attention at something awesomely mysterious.

Someone has been whispering to me in the long dark.
The voice stirs in my heart as a baby stirs in the womb.

Cause of astonishment or admiration.

The light hasn't emerged in ages.
Yet still I sense it pulsing behind the night, aching to burst.

A feeling of doubt or uncertainty.

Are the voice and the light one?
Will the combined force mute me? Blind me?
How can I, weak and struggling, withstand its brilliance?

Miracle.

I don't know how. But I will.
For all this defines wonder.
All this defines you.

Amen.

How to Greet the Night

The strangest thing happened last night: I laughed myself awake.

I was already heading to bed too late as it was. Visions of an early snow and the lingering scent of winter wouldn't leave me. I was snug and cozy beneath the covers. But instead of drifting into la-la land, my brain decided it was playtime.

Cue all sorts of fanciful daydreams about the upcoming holiday season. I pictured arriving at my parents' house under cover of a light December flurry. I saw the Christmas Eve table laid out with more candles than a European cathedral. I could feel my friend's baby bouncing on my knee. I inserted guests who might come and sat them next to relatives I never thought they'd meet. I scripted every dirty joke, every silly action, every loud conversation that could possibly occur with every conceivable combination of friends and family over any number of probable meals. I put myself in such a good mood that I stayed up for another hour, just smiling and castle-building.

What a way to greet the night—not with things that go bump, but with dreams that delight.

Sweet Dreams

You arrive in the moment my eyelids flutter against the deepening dark.

You wait for the moment my muscles forgo their stubborn insistence on perpetual motion.

You reach out at the moment my mind puts aside today's reality and doesn't yet worry about tomorrow's.

You hold me in the moment when only gravity tethers me to my bed.

And with a gentle snip, you release me into weightless joy.

Amen.

Are We There Yet?

A Prayer to End On

Amen, I say to you, amen.
I affirm, I trust, I celebrate you.
I say "so be it" and for once I mean it

Because the wordless prayer I've long desired—
The one I've practiced for,
Striven for,
Hoped for—
I have finally achieved.

Now I know what a wordless prayer sounds like.
It is a keen and whoop, a snore and swoon,
A grumble, a giggle,
A gasp.

Now my soul-voice resonates your whisper.
My muscles recognize your movement.
My intuition revels in your love.

For now I have prayed the most honest prayer—
A prayer beyond language,
A prayer without end.

Amen.

Notes

1. https://www.instagram.com/p/CGQrxJMA65F/?utm_source=ig_web_copy_link.
2. https://legal-dictionary.thefreedictionary.com/beyond+a+reasonable+doubt.
3. https://justfaith.org/wp-content/uploads/2015/04/ES-Step-Two-Session-12.pdf.
4. https://inquiries2015.files.wordpress.com/2008/01/08-5-pa-hope-is-where-your-ass-is.pdf.
5. https://www.ted.com/talks/brene_brown_the_power_of_vulnerability/transcript?language=en.
6. http://colummccann.com/no-literary-olympics/.

Acknowledgments

This little volume required big faith from a lot of people. Here's where I attempt to give them their due.

David Morris of Lake Drive Books, for taking an enthusiastic chance on a debut author. You have such generosity of spirit, and I've already learned so much from you on this publishing journey. Thank you for understanding and elevating my intentions for my work. And to think, I almost didn't do the #PitMad where we met!

Audrey Clare Farley, for guiding the book's arcs and expecting the very best of me; and Stephanie Eagleson, for sharpening my prose and verse.

Jennifer Ryan, Barbara Boehm Miller, Christina Keller, and Emmy Nicklin, my indefatigable critique group and dear friends, for offering invaluable feedback, constant reassurance, and delicious snacks. I hope you enjoy all the chatty bits. And to my friend and fellow writer Priya Chhaya, for encouraging me to create for the sheer joy of it.

Ed Perlman and Mark Farrington, gifted teachers and mentors at The Johns Hopkins University MA in Writing program, for deepening my love of craft.

Charlene Diorka, SSJ, and Eileen Pollack, both instrumental in my spiritual formation, for teaching me how to discern God moving in my life. Special shout-out goes to Eileen for using the term "liminal space" before it became cool.

All my church communities, music ministries, and service activities over the years, for birthing many enduring friendships and blog post topics. Particular gratitude goes to my JustFaith and Minkisi Ministry groups at Our Lady Queen of Peace Catholic Church for sharpening my commitment to social justice. Extra hugs go to Gary Gardner and Kathleen Bashian, fellow writers, who know exactly when to offer ideas, encouragement, or the perfect reading material; and to Cecilia Braveboy, who inspires me with her tenacity and vision.

All the readers of my blog from its earliest days as *Italian Mother Syndrome*, for growing up with me on the internet.

Precious friends from every stage of my life, especially Sue, Emily, Susannah, Jacob, Chandrima, and Brent, for making me laugh and letting me cry, often in the same conversation.

Peggy and Jim, my mother- and father-in-law, for offering an unbelievable amount of childcare so I had time to finish this book (and also sleep). My gratitude knows no bounds.

Francis and Angela, my brother and sister-in-law, for trusting me with big conversations about faith and religion and for cheering me on at every step of my writing journey.

Marie and Pat, my parents, for always believing I could do this. Mom, you are my first and best reader. Dad, you are my first and best editor. Together, you're my best marketers. Thank you for your unconditional love.

James and Vincent, my children, for grounding me in the present. How mind-blowing to have you with me for this milestone—my longest-held visions, parenting and publishing, bursting forth at the same time. I love you.

Matthew, my husband, for cherishing my dreams as if they were your own. You are a literal answered prayer. I thank God every day that we are here, at the same time, together. Thank you, with all my love.

About the Author

Julia Rocchi writes prose, poetry, prayers, and a lot of thank-you notes. With an MA in Writing from Johns Hopkins University, she has garnered multiple story publications and honors, including First Place in the *Saturday Evening Post's* Great American Fiction Contest. Julia also works in nonprofit marketing, facilitates gatherings, and performs improv comedy. As an ENFJ, Enneagram 2, and Cancer sign, she's never met a personality indicator she disagreed with. Julia lives with her family in Arlington, Virginia.